DISCOVERING THE LIFE YOU WERE CREATED FOR !

VOLUME VII

DISCOVERING GOD'S ANOINTING AND GIFTS IN YOUR LIFE

PASTOR DON R. VINING

ISBN 978-1-969865-52-7 (Paperback)
ISBN 978-1-969865-53-4 (Ebook)

Inquiries and Book Orders should be addressed to:

Leavitt Peak Press
17901 Pioneer Blvd Ste L #298,
Artesia, California 90701
Phone #: 2092191548

DEDICATION

Discovering The Life You Were Created For ! is dedicated to my more than forty-five years of business and ministry experience, through all the ups and downs, and all that my family has sacrificed to bring us to this point. To be able to sit back and talk about the adventure we've experienced in serving our God is truly a blessing.

FOREWORD

If I could say anything profound, it would be this: after all these years and experiences, He is truly still the Almighty God.

I am blessed to be a part of His Kingdom's work. It has been an eye-opening journey to realize that before the foundation of the world was formed, God knew me and had plans for me, and not just for me, but for all of mankind.

To think that at the age of six I was expected to die from leukemia, and instead, God healed me and placed upon me the gift of healing for others who would cross my path throughout my life — that alone is humbling.

To think that He would use both positive and negative circumstances, and people from all walks of life, to teach and equip me to be part of His mighty army. The awesome thing is that what He does for one, He does for others. I love celebrating those who came through our ministry, found Christ, and became ministers themselves.

I am equally amazed that it took me until sixty-two years of age to realize that, for over twenty years of writing books, it was all part of His plan, for this particular time. To speak life and understanding into congregations, to help young ministers find their way, and to lift up ministers who have been broken by the systems and the school of hard knocks.

Simply put, the anointing is relentless in moving and shaping our lives unto His glory.

This writing is for every single person who has found their way through our life's work. I thank God for Faith, Family, and Calling.

Pastor Don R. Vining

INTRODUCTION

Discovering The Life You Were Created For ! or anointing of God in your life can be quite a task, unless one learns how to look at the circumstances surrounding it.

Is it possible to discover God's calling through circumstances? Could God be speaking into your life, calling you?

I have asked myself these same questions, and even to this day, I continue to reflect on them.

Over time, I have realized that God often speaks through both the ordinary and extraordinary events of life. Sometimes, He whispers through quiet moments; other times, His direction is revealed in challenges, struggles, or even unexpected blessings. What may seem like a coincidence can often be His divine hand at work, shaping us for the purpose He has prepared.

Discovering The Life You Were Created For ! is not always about hearing an audible voice from heaven. Many times, it begins with recognizing how God has been guiding your steps all along. The people you meet, the doors that open, and even the trials you face may all be part of His way of drawing you closer to your calling.

This book is written to help you see those signs more clearly. My prayer is that as you read these pages, you will find encouragement and insight to recognize the unique way God is speaking to you and leading you into His purpose.

Chapter I

SPIRITUAL GIFTS IMPARTED

Romans 1:11 — *"For I long to see you, that I may impart unto you some spiritual gift, to the end ye may be established."*

The apostle Paul deeply yearned to meet the believers in Rome because he believed that if he could spend time with them, or perhaps lay hands on them, there would be a spiritual impartation. The word *"impart"* in Romans 1:11 is the Greek word metadidomi, which means *to transfer something from one to another*. Paul deliberately chose this word because he was confident that what he carried inside of him could be transferred to the believers in Rome. He believed so strongly in the spiritual deposit within him that he expected it to "rub off" on them if only he could be present in person.

The Meaning of "Gift"

As Paul continued in Romans 1:11, he became very clear about the nature of this impartation. He said he wanted to impart a *"spiritual gift"* to them. The word *"gift"* here is charisma, derived from the word charis, meaning *grace*. When charis becomes charisma, it describes something given freely, a gift imparted by grace.

This is why certain Christians identify themselves as *Charismatics*, emphasizing that they believe in, or strongly value, the gifts of the Holy Spirit as part of their worship and spiritual life.

Historically, the word *charisma* was used to describe the moment when the gods granted supernatural ability, favor, or power to an individual. It conveyed the idea of a gracious gift. In the New

1

Testament, this same word is used to describe the divine enablement believers receive from God. When someone receives a charisma, they are receiving a supernatural donation or empowerment that equips them for a specific work or service in God's Kingdom.

Thus, when Paul declared that he longed to impart a spiritual gift to the Romans, he was essentially saying: *If I can be with you in person, God will release a charisma, a divine empowerment, into your lives.*

To Be Established

Paul further explained his reason for this impartation: *"...that ye may be established"* (Romans 1:11). The word *"established"* comes from the Greek word steridzo, which describes something firm, fixed, and solid, like a strong column that upholds the roof of a house. It also carries the meaning of bracing, reinforcing, or strengthening something that already exists.

In ancient times, *steridzo* was also used in viticulture. Farmers would drive a rod into the ground next to a growing grapevine. The vine would then wrap itself around the rod, gaining support and direction as it climbed upward. This support allowed the vine to flourish and bear large clusters of grapes. The rod didn't change the vine itself, but it gave it the strength and stability needed to grow and bear fruit.

This is exactly what the gifts of the Holy Spirit are designed to do for believers. They establish us, reinforce us, strengthen us, and help us grow in maturity. They provide stability so that we can flourish and bear much fruit.

The Purpose of the Gifts

Spiritual gifts are not given for personal boasting or self-glorification. They are imparted so that the body of Christ may be strengthened and so that individual believers can stand firm in their faith. Just as the grapevine depends on the rod for stability, Christians rely on the spiritual gifts to uphold them as they grow in their walk with Christ.

The end result is not merely personal blessing, but fruitfulness that glorifies Jesus and furthers His Kingdom. Spiritual gifts are, therefore, not optional extras in the Christian life — they are essential tools given by grace to establish and equip us for the work of God.

Chapter II

LOOKING BACK

Again, Romans 1:11 declares, *"For I long to see you, that I may impart to you some spiritual gift."* As I sit here and reflect on my life from childhood, I can clearly see how God has, for a lifetime, been speaking into my heart: *"For I long to see you, that I may impart unto you special gifts (calling/anointing)."* It seems as though God has been equipping me, piece by piece, to fulfill a work for His kingdom.

As early as six years of age, in 1968, God began imparting His special gifts into my life. At that time, I had been very sick. My parents took me to the doctor, only to receive devastating news: I had leukemia. The doctors informed my parents that their little boy would likely die within one year, because there was no known cure at that time.

I remember small details from those days. Each time they took me out of my hospital room in Lake City, Florida, we would cross the street to the produce stand to get a chocolate drink. Yet, every time I was out in the direct sun, my nose would start pouring blood. My parents must have been deeply disappointed and afraid, but all they knew to do was turn to God. They went to church, prayed, and asked the congregation to believe with them that God would give their little boy new blood.

After months of prayer and standing in faith, the head doctors requested to meet with my parents. They probably braced themselves for the worst news. But instead, the doctors told my parents that they had no explanation for what had happened. It was as though some-one had pulled the plug, drained all the poisonous blood out, and

4

given me brand-new blood. From that day, no more treatment was necessary except periodic checkups.

Little did we know, that miracle was only the beginning of God's impartation of special gifts in my life. It's no wonder I have never had a problem asking God for miracles in the lives of others. The Bible says, *"For there is no respect of persons with God"* (Romans 2:11). He doesn't see faces, He sees souls and hearts. What He did for me, He can and will do for others.

From a young age, I often did things ahead of my years, or sometimes just plain crazy things. As a child, I was usually the class clown. Today, I see that same streak in my 14-year-old grandson. He's a chip off the old block, always challenging his abilities and making people laugh. When he and his 14-year-old cousin are together, they're quite the package. Not long ago, he climbed a high chain-link fence at the ballfield, fell, and shattered his elbow, the same injury I had at 13, when I fell off the high slide at school. Recently, he also had knee surgery after roughhousing with his friends. Now I'm going through knee surgery myself, his from youthful foolishness, mine from simply getting older.

Back in first and second grade, I had a strange habit: I would shove pencil erasers or tiny rocks up my nose as far as I could. One day, I got a rock stuck so far up that my mother had to rush me to the hospital. Just before we arrived, I sneezed and the rock flew out. I proudly handed it to my mother and said, "We don't have to go now." While she was relieved, she was also very frustrated. That episode had nothing to do with a calling, it certainly didn't slay any giants, but it was one of many wild stories from my childhood.

Through it all, my mother would often remind me that God had told her He was going to use me. My father, on the other hand, wasn't always so convinced. Sometimes, he thought my antics were more evidence of foolishness than of divine calling. For example, once I stuck the water hose deep into the ground, turned it on, and left it. The next morning, when my dad went out to his truck, the hose was frozen in the ground. He had to cut it off, and let's just say we had a serious "discussion" about that hose.

Another time, when I got home from school, I would use chains to hook up the doghouse to our old International tractor's lift and move it around the yard. Every night, my dog had a new place to sleep until my dad finally told me to quit aggravating the poor animal.

One of the bigger mishaps came when my middle brother and I took my dad's Jon boat and motor to a small lake. At full speed, my brother suddenly threw it in reverse, and the motor flew straight up and sank. Thankfully, we managed to grab the fuel tank, which was still attached, and pull it back into the boat. We hurriedly put it away before Dad got home. About six months later, Dad went fishing, only to discover the motor was frozen solid. That was another "secret" we had to keep.

There was also an old man down the road who owned a John Deere bulldozer. I loved putting on my cowboy hat and hanging out at his shop. One day, I knocked something over, and he called me "a little hemorrhoid." Thinking it was something special, I went around proudly telling people, "I'm a hemorrhoid." One day at a restaurant, I said it in front of my dad, who looked like he could bury me right then and there. Afterward, he explained what it really meant. I was so disappointed, I thought it meant I was important.

In 1976, the Bicentennial year, when I was 14, my dad bought me a 3-speed bicycle. But I had an urge to make it unique. With the help of my friend Tony's dad, who was a well driller, I turned that bike into a chopper. I bought a red, white, and blue banana seat with a sissy bar, some cheap spray paint, and used handlebars and wheels from an old bike. Soon, I had my own Bicentennial Chopper Bicycle. All the kids loved it. My dad, however, was less than impressed. When he found out I had transformed my regular 3-speed into a chopper, he said, "I think you've lost your ever-loving mind!"

Bikes in general caused my dad a lot of grief. My friends and I once tied ropes around our waists and rode our bikes off the dock into the lake. We thought it was great fun, until my dad happened to drive by and realized we could drown if the bikes sank into the mud while tied to us. That ended our water-bike adventures immediately.

Through all these stories, my mother continued to believe God had placed special gifts in my life. My dad, slowly but surely, began to see it too. I worked hard as a young boy. From mowing yards to stocking grocery shelves, pumping gas, making banana splits, and even running a restaurant while my boss ran errands, God was teaching me the special gift of responsibility.

I remember vividly the day I turned 12. My mother took me to get my work permit. Mr. Steele, who owned Forest Grocery, hired me to stock shelves, and before long, I was also operating the cash register. My dad came in one day, saw me behind the register, and said, "What are you doing on that register?" I told him my boss said I could. For once, I think my dad began to realize that maybe God really had spared me from leukemia for a reason.

Fishing trips with my dad also taught me lessons. Once, in my excitement, I stood up when I hooked a fish and nearly tipped over the boat. Minutes later, I accidentally hooked my dad in the ear when I cast my line. That was the end of fishing for the day, but not the end of my lessons in balance, patience, and caution. One of my proudest moments came when I caught a four-pound largemouth bass. My dad was so proud of me then.

Looking back, I see that every detail, the miracle of healing, the wild childhood adventures, the work experiences, even the discipline from my father, were all part of God shaping me, imparting gifts, and preparing me for His calling.

Chapter III

DAD'S VOICE WAS THE VOICE OF GOD THAT I UNDERSTOOD

One day when I got home from school, I had the urge to drive my mother's car while she was out on her afternoon bus route with the public-school system. We had about a one-hundred-and-fifty-foot-long driveway. I climbed into that Pontiac Catalina with its 400-horse engine, backed all the way to the highway, and floored it. Boy, did those tires burn!

About the fourth time down the driveway, something unforgettable happened. Now, you need to understand that my dad was a forest ranger. The work center where he was stationed joined the property we lived on, since we stayed in a government home provided for rangers. One of those times, I ran off the side of the driveway and punched it, digging a hole about six inches deep before the car came back up onto the concrete. By the fourth trip of smoking those tires, I looked over and saw my dad standing in the parking lot at the work center. His arms were crossed, and he was glaring at what was going on.

At that moment, all I could think of was how much he looked like God standing there. I quickly eased the car back into the garage and rushed to cover the holes with pine straw so no one would see them. In my mind, Dad—my "God figure"—was about to kill me. But instead of scolding me immediately, he didn't say a word until dinner time. Then, calmly, he said, "Son, go out and show your mother what you were doing with her car today." I thought for sure she was going to whip me until I couldn't stand.

Early Lessons in Work and Responsibility

At the age of 15, my dad showed me dirt roads through the woods where I could drive to nearby neighborhoods to cut lawns. For years I had used push mowers, but eventually I bought an old Craftsman riding mower, along with an electric weed eater, hedge clippers, and a blower. By mid-summer, with my own money, I was able to purchase a 1969 Chevy Stepside—six-cylinder, three-speed on the column—for $600. I was so proud of my little business, thriving entirely from what I had earned myself.

One of the bigger lessons I learned about business came from my boss at the grocery store. On occasion, he would go crabbing and pay me $50 to sort the crabs. That's where I believe God was showing me that in business, sometimes you *will* get pinched. Those crabs were relentless, and they knew how to get your attention!

First Job, First Firing

At 16, I worked at Winn-Dixie and later at Kash & Karry, where I experienced being fired for the very first time. I would wake up before dawn, head to work at 5 a.m. to unload grocery trucks until 7 a.m., clock out, then go to school, and return to work again from 3 p.m. to 7 p.m. The problem was that I lived 20 miles from work and struggled to arrive on time each morning.

One week, after being late twice, my boss warned me that if I was late again, he would fire me. A friend who lived only five miles from work suggested I stay with him so I wouldn't risk being late. It sounded like a good plan. The next morning, everything was going smoothly, and we were set to be 15 minutes early, until a train stopped us and delayed us by 10 minutes.

When I walked into work, my boss was waiting at the door in his pajamas. He looked straight at me and said, "You're fired." To make things worse, he also fired my friend, the very one who was trying to help me. I remember my friend slamming the pricing gun down, parts flying everywhere, and all I could do was laugh. Looking back, I believe it was the first time the spirit of laughter came over me. Perhaps God gave me that gift of humor because He knew I would need it working with people.

I quickly found another job at K-Mart, assigned to the toy department. But I was determined not to let my dad know I had been fired. He always taught me that my word was my bond, and when you take a job, you give it your best.

Employee 99

At K-Mart, I was known as Employee 99. Whenever they called that number over the PA system, I came running to whatever task needed to be done. The pay was $3.15 per hour, and though it wasn't much, I took pride in doing my part.

One day, they called me to the front entrance with a shovel and mop bucket. When I arrived, three assistant managers were standing there laughing at a pile of dog mess where a customer's pet had relieved itself. They told me to clean it up while they mocked me.

It wasn't that I thought I was too good to clean it, but the humiliation of being laughed at while doing the job cut deep. I was already self-conscious, nearly six feet tall, weighing only 120 pounds, and wearing a goofy tie. At that point, I was close to quitting. But once again, God was preparing to show me something greater.

Discovering Another Gift

The very next day, on my day off, God opened a new door. A man named Lou Bateman, who owned a dump truck, stopped me on the road near my house. Knowing my dad did tractor work in the community, Lou asked if I wanted to earn $20 to spread a load of dirt in someone's yard. I jumped at the opportunity.

After seeing the quality of my work, Lou paid me $40 to spread two more loads and offered to spread my name around if I wanted to do tractor work in the community. That one job changed my entire direction. K-Mart was paying me $25.20 before taxes for eight hours of work, while I had just made $60 in three hours. That was a no-brainer! I quit being Employee 99 and stepped into something new.

The Tractor Business and God's Favor

When my dad later asked about my K-Mart job, I told him I was going into the tractor business. He looked at me and asked, "How are you going into business with no tractor?" I replied, "I've got yours. We're family."

And so, for the next 10 years, I operated in that business. I did hundreds of jobs, leaving early in the morning, often stopping at the Earlybird Restaurant where my dad and local men gathered to share jokes. They never treated me differently because I was young, but instead encouraged me. I learned more about people, business, and God's faithfulness during those years than I could have imagined.

There were mishaps like the time I ran over a shallow septic tank and caved it in. We thought we would never get that tractor out of the mess, and the smell lingered for weeks. But even through challenges, the business thrived. The *Forest Gazette* even wrote a story about me a 16-year-old kid riding up and down the roads, impressing people with my tractor skills. They called me the "Forest Redneck."

Family, Faith, and Calling

During those years, I gained a wife, now my partner of 45 years, two daughters (now ages 37 and 40), and five grandchildren who all live nearby. Looking back, I can see that God was shaping my character and developing the gifts He had placed inside me.

I also taught Sunday School and led the Christian Service Brigade for boys at our church, teaching them camping, fire-building, tool sharpening, and compass hiking. Yet even then, I didn't see myself as a man with a calling or anointing. I just knew I loved being around people and wanted to make a positive difference in their lives.

CHAPTER IV

A New Name

The Promise of a New Name

The Bible says, *"To him that overcometh I will give a new name."*
Very often in ancient society, a person received a "new name" when he achieved a new status or advanced to a higher level of society. The bestowal of a new name normally accompanied a person's elevation, ennoblement, or social promotion. With it came rank, privilege, and frequently, the right of inheritance. That new name marked a distinct change in an individual's status, one that could potentially impact his lineage for generations to come.

Old Testament Examples of a New Name

We see this pattern many times in Scripture. The Bible records numerous accounts of God conferring new names upon His people whenever they underwent life-changing spiritual transformations.
Take, for instance, the Old Testament examples of Abraham and Sarah. When God changed Abram's name to Abraham, it marked a new beginning in his life, a spiritual advancement or elevation. The name Abram means *father*, reflecting his role as the head of his household. However, when Abram entered into a covenant with God, his name was changed to Abraham, meaning *father of many nations*. This new name memorialized the covenant between God and Abraham and reflected his new, God-ordained status in life (Genesis 17:4).

As further affirmation of His promise, God also changed the name of Abraham's wife. Sarai, which means *quarrelsome*, was changed to Sarah, meaning *princess*. Genesis 17:15–16 records this event: *"And God said unto Abraham, As for Sarai thy wife, thou shalt not call her name Sarai, but Sarah shall her name be. And I will bless her, and give thee a son also of her: yea, I will bless her, and she shall be a mother of nations; kings of people shall be of her."* The new names of Abraham and Sarah did not in themselves transform them, but they reflected the divine change God was performing within them. It marked the end of one chapter and the beginning of a new one.

Consider that Abraham was 99 years old and Sarah 90 when God gave them new names. Their story shows us that it is never too late for God to bring transformation and open a new chapter in our lives.

Jacob Becomes Israel

Another powerful example is found in the story of Jacob. The name *Jacob* means *supplanter*, pointing to the mischievousness of his early character. Even at birth, Jacob came out of the womb grasping his brother Esau's heel, revealing the intense competition between the brothers.

But after Jacob's life-changing encounter with the angel at Peniel, God gave him a new name. Genesis 32:27–28 records: *"And he said unto him, What is thy name? And he said, Jacob. And he said, Thy name shall be called no more Jacob, but Israel: for as a prince hast thou power with God and with men, and hast prevailed."*

The name *Israel* means *one who prevails with God* or *God rules*. It signified Jacob's surrender and transformation. Like Abraham and Sarah, the new name itself did not make him different, but it marked the moment when one chapter permanently closed and a new destiny opened, one that would impact the entire history of God's people.

New Names in the New Testament

This divine principle continues in the New Testament. For example, Simon received the new name Peter after his revelation of Christ (Matthew 16:18). The name Peter, from the Greek *petra* meaning *rock*, marked a transformational moment in his discipleship. Today, he is remembered not as Simon, but as Peter, the rock upon which Christ would build His church.

Likewise, Saul of Tarsus underwent a radical transformation after his encounter with Jesus on the road to Damascus. Once an arrogant persecutor of Christians (Philippians 3:4), Saul received a new name, Paul, meaning *small* or *humble*. On the other side of his divine encounter, he was clothed with a new identity. From that moment forward, he was no longer remembered as Saul the persecutor, but as Paul the apostle of Christ.

Our New Identity in Christ

Each of these new names, Abraham, Sarah, Israel, Peter, and Paul, marked profound new beginnings and deep transformations of character. Likewise, when we surrender our lives to Jesus Christ, He redefines who we are.

Although our earthly names may not have changed, the Lord placed a new spiritual identity upon us. We are no longer the same people we used to be. In Christ, old things have passed away and all things have become new. Our "new name" may not be written on paper, but it is inscribed upon our hearts, testifying that we belong to Him.

Chapter V

WHAT IS YOUR SPIRITUAL NAME?

We already know that my worldly, carnal, or *before Christ as Savior* name was "Hemorrhoid"! Recently, I began to ponder this deeply and asked myself: *What name would God give me today to describe who I am in His eyes?*

In search of perspective, I texted my pastor friend, Frederick Shumba, in Zimbabwe, Africa, and asked him: *If you were going to rename Don R. Vining with a biblical influence, based on what you know about me over the past 20 years, what name would you give me?*

Now, I was expecting one simple word. But I was totally blown away by his response. He wrote:

"I would call you Mountain of Goodness or Revival. You have made such an influence, starting from your own family. Look at your kids and grandchildren. You are such a hardworking person and an amazing giver. There are churches in Zimbabwe that bear your name, buildings and wells that could not have been without you. You are an incredible inspiration to many. You have made a significant contribution to my ministry, brother!"

Can we just pause here for a moment to reflect on God's power to redeem and rename for the sake of His Kingdom?

Early Struggles with Identity

Around the age of 26, I really began to think about working with the youth in our church. Up to that point in my life, I was simply "Donnie."

But then one day I overheard two older men in the church hall-way talking. As I passed them and went just around the corner, one of them said, *"He may be a daddy, but he will never be a good father."*

Those words cut deep. Their impression of me was colored by the fact that I was always the life of the party. Yes, the kids, even the youth, loved my personality, and there were always kids hanging around our house. But to them, my past overshadowed any potential they thought I might have.

At the time, our church was in need of a youth pastor. I went to the pastor and asked if I could serve with the youth, explaining that I already had a job and didn't need to be paid. I still didn't know much about a *calling* then, but I did know I had a desire.

A Cry from the Heart

I remember singing the song:

> *If You can use anything, Lord, You can use me.*
> *Take my hand, take my feet, touch my heart,*
> *and speak through me.*

Looking back now, I realize that this was my cry to God, and His invitation to me. I would inwardly weep whenever we sang that song. Even now at 62, it still grips my heart with the same power.

Yet when I approached my pastor, he told me they needed someone with a degree for the job. To me, it felt like he was saying I wasn't "good enough" for God to use.

Seeds of Influence

But even when leaders overlooked me, God was still at work. There was a lady in the church, one of the pastor's key helpers, who had four children. One of her sons practically lived at my house and worked with me. At age 15, he asked me to teach him how to operate a tractor.

Today, at age 45, he runs one of the largest construction companies in our area, doing millions of dollars in contracts every year. His sons now work with him, one managing their restaurant, the other managing part of the construction company, while his wife oversees the office.

Just imagine what would have been lost if I had listened to that pastor's words that I wasn't "good enough" or that I needed a degree.

An Open Door with the Youth

A full year passed, and the church still had not found a youth pastor. So I asked his mother, Shirley, to petition the pastor to let us work with the youth for just the summer. He finally agreed.

At that time, there were 25 young people in the group. In just three months, attendance grew to more than 50! For the first time, I began to sense that perhaps this desire was more than just me; it might be a God-thing.

Yet eventually, the church hired an "educated" youth pastor. Within the first year, he misused the church credit card to buy himself a $200 pair of shoes, and the youth group declined. I remember telling the pastor that it looked like he had hired a "piece of paper with no values." I told him plainly that the church would have been better off financially and spiritually, using those of us who were uneducated but faithful.

Rejection and the Prophet's Dilemma

I once asked one of the councilmen why the pastor resisted letting me work in youth ministry. He told me: *"It will never work because you are a homeboy. You won't be accepted. Haven't you heard? A prophet is without honor in his hometown."*

Even Jesus was rejected in Nazareth, where many dismissed His teachings (Matthew 13:58). I thought to myself, *"I'm not even asking to be on paid staff — I just want to work with the youth!"*

17

Stewards of Grace

Scripture tells us:

> "As every man hath received the gift, even so minister the same one to another, as good stewards of the manifold grace of God."
> — 1 Peter 4:10

Every person has been given grace-gifts, not earned, but divinely imparted by God's mercy. These gifts are not for boasting. They are meant to reveal God to man. You and I carry these powerful gifts inside us, waiting for us to take ownership and release them for the benefit of others.

The word *stewards* in this verse comes from the Greek *oikonomos* — a compound of *oikos* (house) and *nomos* (law). In Greek culture, this word described the household manager of a wealthy estate. This person had been found faithful and was entrusted with overseeing the property, resources, and finances of the family.

In the same way, when God places His grace-gifts inside us, He is entrusting us with His own treasures. He expects us to be faithful managers of them, using them on time, meeting the needs of others, and bringing glory to His name.

Faithful with the Gifts

When we take all this into consideration, 1 Peter 4:10 essentially teaches us that every single one of us has received something from God. We must recognize it, embrace it, and faithfully use it.

Too many sit waiting for some "perfect moment" to step out and use their gifts. But the truth is, God already gave us permission when He placed those gifts within us. Waiting endlessly leads only to frustration.

I've seen this time and time again in my own life and in ministry: Those who wait for a fantasy-like moment often miss opportunities right in front of them. But those who recognize God's deposit and act on it find fulfillment and fruitfulness.

God has entrusted us with **spiritual treasure**. Now He calls us to be faithful stewards of it, releasing it, managing it, and using it for His glory and the good of others.

CHAPTER VI

NO TIME TO WASTE

I encourage you, if you've been waiting on a special moment to step out and use your grace-gifts for God, don't waste any more time! The Holy Spirit within you has already enabled and empowered you, so start making the most of your divine equipment that's just waiting to be released!

A Personal Confession

I have a surprise for every reader. For over 35 years of ministry and 62 years of living on this earth, NOT one time have I heard God audibly say, *"I have called you to ministry."* But at the same time, I felt it deep within me to be so.

I used to hear the old timers say, *"my knower knows."* And let me tell you, with everything in me, I know that the Creator, the Almighty God, the Healer, and the Savior has placed a call on my life to spread the Good News, that Jesus Christ loves a lost and dying world!!

This wasn't something I conjured up or forced. God was preparing me in many, many ways with spiritual gifts to do a work in His kingdom. And as I look back, I can see clearly how He was implementing His plan piece by piece.

God's Perfect Timing

Timing matters with God.

When it became clear that I would not be working with the youth in my local church, something else was already in motion. At the same time, an optometrist in town closed his office to step into full-time pastoring.

Now, get this, his father was my pastor when I was a child. He had pastored at our church before the very pastor who wouldn't let me work with the youth. This same man had also been the pastor who gave my older brother the opportunity to preach his first message.

And here's the full circle: his son, the optometrist, was about to plant a new work across town and was looking for a youth pastor. Timing!

He was also the pastor who gave me the opportunity to preach my very first message. Wow, if that isn't God! One pastor didn't want me, and the other couldn't wait to have me.

I served there for two years. We started with two youth, and within six months, we had 43, not because of a degree or special program, but simply by loving and spending time with those kids.

The Scooby-Doo Van

I literally purchased a Scooby-Doo van — yes, with brown shag carpet on the walls! I'd take one direction picking up youth, while my wife went in another direction.

By then, I knew beyond any doubt that God had called me into ministry. And when I thought back, I remembered that this process started way back when I was just six years old, dying of leukemia. God wasn't finished yet.

Remember, we are learning together how to identify with God's calling on your life.

Wildwood: A New Assignment

When it was time to move on, I listed three churches I wanted to visit. The first was the Sonset Park COG in Wildwood, FL.

Again, God's timing.

My family had known the pastor for years before, when he served as an evangelist. We walked in and sat midway down the center aisle with about 400 people in attendance. The pastor and his brothers were well known in music and evangelism.

As the pastor played the Hammond B-3 organ before service, he suddenly stopped, came down the center aisle, and right up to me.

"Don Vining, what in the world are you doing down here?" he asked.

I said, "Well, actually, I'm looking for a church to get involved with the youth."

He replied, "Well, let's get together this week. I'm looking for a youth pastor."

"It pays to listen."

The night before, out of three churches, I had told my wife we'd go to Williston COG. But the next morning, I felt in my gut that Wildwood was where we needed to be. My wife said, "This isn't the way to Williston." And I said, "I know, but I just feel we're supposed to go to Wildwood."

Only God could have orchestrated this. Out of 400 people, that pastor walked straight to me, someone he barely knew, and invited me into ministry.

Healing in Wildwood

That church became my first paid staff position. As I write this, I'm almost in tears remembering how God wrapped me with special gifts ever since I was six years old.

The church majored in high praise, worship, and healing miracle services. With God having already healed me of leukemia, it was no small thing that He placed me in a church where the miraculous was expected and celebrated.

I'll never forget one healing service: they brought in a man in cowboy boots who couldn't walk or stand on his own. They carried him onto the platform. The pastor told us to pray like our lives were on the line. As the choir sang *"Our God is an Awesome God,"* the man suddenly began moving his legs. Then, out of nowhere, he broke into the most beautiful dance I had ever seen.

They carried him in, but he ran out under his own strength!

That was just one of many testimonies of weekly healings. Week after week, I sat in awe, being spiritually fed while ministering to the youth.

A Moment of Comfort

One Sunday, a guest singer was ministering. I was on the balcony beside a tough country boy named Leonard, who didn't say much.

At one point, the guest speaker stopped playing the piano and said, *"Sometimes we Christians just say too much. Instead, embrace the person next to you and let virtue flow from your spirit to theirs."*

What no one knew was that I was struggling, feeling out of my league in that church. I couldn't sing, I wasn't much of a preacher, and I often felt unqualified.

But when Leonard embraced me, it felt like God Himself was holding me. That moment carried me. Leonard Power is still my friend to this very day.

Preaching Under Pressure

When the pastor hired me, he introduced me to the former youth leader, who told me, *"The first Sunday night of each month is youth service, and the youth pastor preaches to the entire congregation."*

I thought, *"Oh my Lord, I have to preach next Sunday."* I had only preached once before!

I was so nervous. And when I read my text, I said: *"I am reading from the King James VIRGIN..."* instead of "Version." The whole church caught it. You could hear my sister's laughter over everyone else's.

But I pressed through. I delivered the message, and the altars filled with people crying out to God. So many thanked me for a timely word.

Youth on Fire

We began with 26 kids and grew to over 100 in weekly attendance. The pastor supported us in renting an old theater downtown. We raised funds, paid rent and utilities, even hired a part-time music minister to build a worship team.

It felt like pastoring my own church. We traveled to different churches holding youth rallies, and God moved powerfully.

The pastor also supported me through a 9-month ministerial internship program and endorsed me for the Exhorter License. I became a credentialed minister. He often introduced me as "Don Vining, a man who marches to the beat of his own drum."

After four years in Wildwood, it was time for the next assignment.

More Experience, More Gifts

Another pastor I had known from years earlier, while working with the Christian Service Brigade boys' club, was starting a new church.

By this point, I had five years of ministry experience and credentials. He asked me to serve for one year to help launch the new work.

We rented an old auto parts building, renovated it, and grew to 100 in attendance. I completed my one-year commitment and also achieved my Minister's License Certificate.

Now I had over seven years of hands-on experience, was licensed to pastor my own church, and had served on the State Youth Board for two years.

Hot Dogs Everywhere

Serving on the youth board was a great honor, and it brought some unforgettable memories. At one camp with 400 kids, I was asked to help prepare lunch.

We boiled 500 hot dogs and loaded them into pans in the bed of my truck. But when I turned a corner, two pans slid out and hot dogs rolled across the parking lot! Kids screamed, I was stunned, and we had to run to three grocery stores to buy replacements.

In the end, it gave us something to laugh about every time we got together.

Preparing for the Next Journey

As my time on the youth board wrapped up, I knew God was calling me to plant a church. With years of experience, credentials, and countless stories of God's faithfulness, I carried not just lessons but treasured memories into the next journey He had prepared for me.

CHAPTER VII

MORE DETERMINED THAN EVER

Now I can tell you that the past seven years have had their share of bumps in the road. I feel like I had to fight on almost every level (more on the fight later). However, the bumps and bruises had been worth it.

They made me feel more called, more determined, and more favorable with God to do His work. Not only did I beat the cancer of leukemia at the age of six, but I also beat all the other cancers that came through men and their ugliness.

Little did I know I hadn't seen anything yet. Thank God He gave me the special gift of conquering obstacles. Every bump and bruise helped me identify and understand my calling.

When Man Closes a Door

So, back to the pastor, the thorn who didn't want us to work in his church with the youth, some seven years back.

Let me give you some context. Our organization has an **Executive Office** that oversees all churches. Under the executive branch, every state has a **State Office** with an overseer who oversees all local churches. Then each state is divided into regions with **District Pastors** who oversee the churches in their area. And finally, you have the **local church.**

Well, after finishing at our last appointment, we moved back to our original district. The very pastor who hadn't wanted me working with the youth was now the **District Pastor** over the churches in our area. That meant everything happening on a local level had to go through him.

I'm taking my time here to show you this truth: when man closes a door, God can and will reopen the same door in order for you to succeed with your assignment.

The Call to Plant a Church

I felt God tugging at my heart to plant a new church in our district. The problem was, the district overseer wasn't going to allow me to do it. He refused to acknowledge my seven years of success and the fact that I had paid my dues to be credentialed. In his eyes, I was still just *"Donnie the kid."*

But God had a plan.

One Saturday, while I was in the swimming pool, my phone rang. I couldn't believe it, it was the **State Overseer of Florida, Raymond Crowley.**

He said: *"Brother Vining, I'm told you would like to start a church in your area."*

I answered, *"Yes, I would, but I don't have the support of the District Overseer. For some reason, I just can't get past him."*

The State Overseer replied: *"The buck stops with me, and I'll deal with the district pastor. There comes a time for every man to stand on his own two feet. Turn in the request in writing, and I'll get you approved. Let's get to work with your vision to build a church."*

Again, God's timing and anointing are so important to flowing and identifying in the gifts and calling of God. With this approval, we planted a church and pastored there for over 25 years.

From Living Room to Storefront

Starting a new church was both exciting and challenging. It all begins as a **Mission Work** and later becomes an organized local church.

We held our first meeting in our home to see who would be interested. Out of 50 invitations, 23 people showed up, and all committed to the process.

Our first hurdle was finding a place to meet. We rented a bingo hall on Sundays just to get started. That first service had 23 in attendance. My sister and I sang old hymns with an older gentleman playing piano. Boy, that was something to behold; neither one of us could really sing, but God was in it.

After six weeks, we moved into a small storefront. Of course, we needed carpet, paint, a sound system, chairs, everything. Once we grew to 40 people, we had another problem: no room for the children.

So I borrowed an old military tent from a friend, and my wife held the children's church in it. Boy, was it dusty and Florida hot. Several times storms blew it down, and we'd put it back up again and again. Still, it was an exciting time to watch God move in people's lives.

Creative Fundraising and God's Provision

We knew we needed a larger building soon. One Saturday, during a yard sale, my dad and I were driving around buying items at garage sales to resell. We passed a vacant metal building, and my dad said, *"There's a building you might rent."*

We stopped and met the man inside, a businessman who had once attended my old home church. Through a few discussions, he not only agreed to rent to us, but he also **loaned the church $20,000 to renovate, later sold us the building and 10 acres, and even held the mortgage.**

Wow — God was so good.

Expansion Through Unlikely Means

After two years, we needed more space again. A member told me about a **6,400 sq. ft. metal building** for sale for $5,000. It would need to be torn down and moved 80 miles to our property.

I called the owner and explained our need, saying, *"Could you use a tax credit?"*

He agreed to donate the building as a tax write-off!

Then I found a mover, **Mr. Piggy's Transport Service.** When he learned what the owner was doing for the church, he agreed to deliver the building for only $400.

What a blessing!

Toilets, Golf Carts, and Miracles

We still needed funds to cover costs. One day, while exiting the interstate, I noticed a pile of toilets behind a hotel.

My wife said, *"You're not..."* and I said, *"Oh yes, I am!"*

The maintenance man gave them to me. I lined them up in front of our church and sold them for $1,200, enough to cover the delivery fee.

Later, I bought a golf cart for $2,500 and sold it for $6,000 to buy a lighted church sign.

God was teaching me to be resourceful and reminding me that His provision can come from the most unexpected places.

Trading Up to Greater Things

A friend of mine, who built metal buildings, offered to take our **80x80 building** in trade plus $23,000, and in return, he provided and erected a brand-new **12,000 sq. ft. building.**

After two years, we had a **500-seat sanctuary with offices.** Later, we added a **17,000 sq. ft. Family Life Building** that housed a preschool with more than 100 children. We even launched a series of recordings for television.

The stage was set to go big!

A Turning Point

But now, I need to talk about the unbelievable.

As I write this, it's 2:37 a.m., and I have a lump in my belly the size of a grapefruit because of what I feel compelled to share.

What comes next has nothing to do with God, but everything to do with man's failure.

CHAPTER VIII

IT'S ABOUT TO GET RAW!!

I want to be transparent here. This would be a great time for you, the reader, to move away from all distractions and pay close attention to the heart of the writer/pastor.

If there is any way thus far that I have made it sound like ministry and calling are easy, I will have to say it is anything but easy. I learned a long time ago that the Devil, your spiritual enemy, hates God the Creator, and he hates and despises any and everyone that does a work for God.

A Battle from the Beginning

I was called before I was in my mother's womb.

(Jeremiah 1:5 New Living Translation — "I knew you before I formed you in your mother's womb. Before you were born, I set you apart and appointed you as my prophet to the nations.")

The devil knew it and despised it. No wonder I had leukemia at the age of six. He tried to kill me then, and he still tries to kill my anointing and ministry.

I learned that more experienced, "mature" men with a calling on their own life could sometimes be insensitive and inattentive so as to miss what God might be calling others to. It taught me to pay attention and listen with spiritual ears.

Wounds from My Home Church

From the very church that I grew up in, you would have thought the pastor would be proud that I felt called to God.

I sat tearfully in his office telling him what I was feeling. When I had finished, he looked across his desk at me and said:

"If you feel that God is calling you to ministry, then you should turn and run like HELL in the other direction."

Boy, did my tears dry up. You could have heard a pin drop in that room. I was TOTALLY BLOWN AWAY by his response. I know what he meant was that ministry isn't easy, but my Lord, could he have found another way to say it?

I had to nearly beg him to let me work with the youth. He was the very one I overheard in that hallway telling his friend that I might be a daddy, but I would never be a good father.

Those words pierced deep. Words from a leader you once admired can wound the heart in ways no enemy ever could.

A Rocky Start in Ministry

When we went to the new church across town, if we weren't scared enough, the very first service there, the pastor introduced my wife and me as the new volunteer youth workers. The very next thing he said was that he was resigning as pastor and moving on.

AGAIN — TOTALLY BLOWN AWAY.

His replacement literally made fun of almost everything we tried to do. The good news is, despite the resistance, we grew from two to forty-three youth in six months. That was God showing His hand, not man's.

Painful Lessons Along the Way

The next church hired us on staff, where I really gained experience I am still grateful for. But at about the three-and-a-half-year mark, an evangelist came through and made a sexual pass at one of the young boys in our group. (That young boy is now a full-time pastor with a beautiful family.)

When I met with my pastor/boss and told him what happened, he said we should just leave it alone and move instead of causing trouble in the church.

Again — TOTALLY BLOWN AWAY.

We felt we couldn't stay a part of that church, so within six months we moved on.

At our next assignment, the pastor only had his exhorter certificate. When I asked him to sign my application to take the License test, he refused. He said he couldn't have me with a higher credential than he had.

Literally everything I did to help the ministry succeed, he took credit for and said he had done.

AGAIN — TOTALLY BLOWN AWAY.

After fulfilling our one-year commitment at his church, we moved on once again.

Battles with Leadership

As you read earlier, I also had my battles with the district pastor who was leading the church I grew up in. Honestly, I wasn't a bad person. It was simply that my childhood pastor was upset with the state office for allowing the church across town to be planted in his district.

He told me flat-out that I would never do anything in his church if I supported the church he didn't like.

Wow, what a story. I cannot even begin to tell you the effect this had on my family: the hurt, the tears, and the pain, all from just wanting to be used by God.

So many times, I just wanted to quit.

Staff Issues: Blessings and Battles

As I previously stated, our church ministry was at an all-time high. We had hired many full-time staff and workers for the preschool, twenty-plus employees.

Once we completed the Family Life Building, I came back with our certificate of occupancy. (I never even mentioned all of the battles with the Fire Marshal, Zoning Department, Building Department, and Health Department!)

I immediately met with my staff to celebrate this great milestone. I said to them: *"All we have done for nearly ten years is build buildings, but now we are going to build people."*

Every last one of them looked like a calf staring at a new gate. Right then, I thought: *"Houston, we have a problem."*

I remember telling my wife that same day that I was both so happy and very sad at the same time.

From there, things became rocky. The music person, after many battles over following the vision of the church, left for another church just five miles down the road, and took the entire choir and most of the musicians with them.

The youth minister wanted to pastor elsewhere. Another staff member working with young married couples was battling serious marriage issues of their own.

I hired a semi-retired pastor for hospital visitation, only to find he wanted a paycheck more than ministry. I hired a seasoned youth minister who soon confessed that he didn't want to work with youth anymore because they "drove him crazy." Another youth hire revealed he had severe asthma and couldn't keep up with the activities.

I could go on and on with staff disappointments.

Now, to be fair, these issues stretched over twenty years, but they were still issues. And they wore me down.

Financial Strain and Loss

The economy was about to take a huge hit. I went to the bank and asked them to rewrite our mortgage for more favorable terms.

They basically said there was nothing they could do to help; this was before the financial issues even hit.

I asked our state office for help, and they told me they would "pray for us." That didn't make sense since their name was also on the deed along with the local church.

After more struggles, I made the hard decision to give the property and buildings back to the bank. We rented a storefront to meet in, which brought our attendance to around eighty. Later, I personally purchased a building that the church could rent for cheaper than we were paying. But over the next four years, attendance dwindled to around twenty-five.

Final Years and Deep Loss

After twenty-five years of pastoring, with so many great memories mixed with disappointments, life hit even harder.

My very best friend died in a motorcycle accident after we had ridden together all day. My dad passed away three years later. Our mothers passed within two weeks of each other.

By that time, we felt we just needed to walk away, and so we did.

I said, like Jeremiah, that I would not speak of pastoring again.

But after some time, Jeremiah also said the gospel was like a fire shut up in his bones. And here we are, fast-forward three years after closing the doors. Now, in 2025, I say the same: *this calling, this anointing, this word is like a fire shut up in my bones.*

Looking Back with Hope

I am sorry to have shared all the bad, because truthfully, there is far more good than bad. Most of my hardest decisions were made when I was angry and burned out, more exhausted than I ever realized until it was all gone.

But even in the pain, there is still much good. At least twenty people from our youth groups through the years are serving in full-time ministry. Hundreds have found divine healing in their lives.

I am now writing my seventh book with great clarity about what God wants said.

These are the last days we are living in, and if we're going to do anything for the Kingdom, now is the time!

Still Anointed

I can tell you that the gifts and calling of God are without repentance.

(Romans 11:29 — "For the gifts and calling of God are without repentance.")

The gifts and calling of God are not subject to a change of mind on God's part. You may be in the ministry and anointed. You may be on the sidelines. You may be taking a long sabbatical, but you're still anointed.

You may be re-entering ministry after a long break. You are still anointed by God, who called you according to His Word.

You just cannot get away from what He has laid on your life.

It truly is a fire shut up in your bones.

A New Name

I asked another pastor friend of mine, Rudy Roberts, if he were going to rename Don R. Vining based on what he knew about my life and ministry, what would his biblical name be?

Immediately, he said: **"TRAILBLAZER!"**

CHAPTER IX

BEFORE I WAS BORN, GOD KNEW ME!!

God's Knowledge Before Birth

God, through the Holy Spirit, spoke to my mother when I was born that He was going to use me by His anointing. So there must have been something, even before I was in my mother's womb that God already knew. That knowledge allowed Him to speak directly to my mother at the very moment of my birth.

God told Jeremiah in **Jeremiah 1:5**:

> *"Before I formed you in the belly I knew you; and before you came forth out of the womb, I sanctified you, and I ordained you a prophet unto the nations."*

In this, one can easily see the doctrine of predestination. But let me clarify: it is not that Jeremiah was denied the power of choice, nor that he was forced into a certain course of action. Rather, it was God's **foreknowledge**, His ability to know Jeremiah's heart and path before Jeremiah even lived it. This is the same principle we are exploring in learning how to identify God's calling on our own lives.

The Depth of Jeremiah 1:5

This verse is one of the most profound in all of Scripture because it speaks to the **fundamental truth of human identity and purpose**.

When God spoke to Jeremiah, He revealed that before he was even conceived, God had a plan for his life. This is no small detail. It means that God knows us intimately and has a divine purpose for each of us long before we ever take our first breath.

This assurance should comfort anyone who has ever felt forgotten, overlooked, or lost. We are not accidents. We are not random. We are **intentionally created** by the hand of God, carefully formed and prepared for roles we are meant to play in this world.

The implications of this truth stretch far beyond birth. God's knowledge of us transcends time itself. Before our parents dreamed of us, before we were given a name, before we cried our first cry — God already had us in His heart.

So when doubts and fears come, and they always do, this verse reassures us: **God knows who we are, where we are, and where He is taking us.**

A Calling for Everyone

Jeremiah's calling was to be a prophet, but the principle applies to all of us. You may not stand in a pulpit or deliver prophecy, but God still has a calling that is unique to you. Some are called to teach, some to raise godly children, some to care for the hurting, some to lead through business or service.

Bottom line: Many are called, but all were known before the foundations of the world were formed.

So I know this: before I was in the womb, before I was born, God already knew me and had a purpose for me. We are anointed by the power of God, and if we listen closely, we can spiritually hear His voice guiding us. To realize this is liberating. It explains why, even when we feel beaten down or wasted, we cannot quit.

As Jeremiah once said, *"This word is like fire shut up in my bones."*

John 2:24-25 But Jesus did not commit himself unto them, because he knew all men, vrs.25 And needed not that any should testify of man: for he knew what was in man.

The Word and the Armor of God

The Bible says, *"Wherever the soles of your feet tread is yours."* (Deuteronomy 11:24)

And in **Ephesians 6:15**, when speaking of the whole armor of God, it declares: *"And your feet shod with the preparation of the gospel of peace."*

I began to ask myself: *What is the Gospel?*

Romans 1:16 answers:

> *"For I am not ashamed of the Gospel of Christ, for it is the power of God to everyone who believes — to the Jew first and also to the Greek."*

So if I am walking daily with the full armor of God, then it means I am walking with the very power of God strapped to my feet like shoes. That realization alone is enough to make me more confident in the calling God has placed on my life.

The more I understand my calling, the more I see that God has already equipped me for everything I will face.

The All-Sufficient Word

I want to pause here to talk about **The All-Sufficient Word of the Living God**.

If He knew me before the foundation of the world, then the only way I can truly know Him is through His Word. It is His Word that reveals His heart and His plan for me. It is His Word that confirms the anointing He placed on me. And it is His Word that fuels the fire inside me.

Yes, there are times when I feel down, discouraged, or out of step with the Spirit. But God never lets me stay there. He keeps calling, keeps reminding, keeps stirring me. That's why I can boldly say: I know that I know that I am called.

Looking Back Over My Life

Honestly, I could fill volumes just talking about God's hand on my life for these 62 years. From the time I was a child, there were moments that showed there was something different, something God was doing in me.

Even my mother, at my birth, knew by the Spirit that I was set apart. It wasn't just her natural intuition as a mother. It was God Himself whispering into her spirit. That's the difference between the human and the spiritual.

The Ability to Hear God

But here's the challenge: Sometimes God is talking, yet we don't or can't hear His voice.

Matthew 13:15 says:

> *"For the hearts of this people have grown dull. Their ears are hard of hearing, and their eyes they have closed, lest they should see with their eyes and hear with their ears, lest they should understand with their hearts and turn, so that I should heal them."*

Years ago, I remember buying Q-Tips, dipping them in anointing oil, and handing them out to the congregation. I told the people to clean their ears so they could once again hear the voice of God clearly. Now, I don't know if the Q-Tips made a physical difference, but I do know what the Word says: **"It's the anointing that makes the difference."**

And I can report, after that simple act of faith, it seemed like the congregation's spiritual eyes and ears were wide open. Their worship, their attentiveness, and their hunger for God's Word were never the same.

Anointing for Every Believer

Every believer carries an anointing.
In **1 Samuel 16:13**, it says:

> *"Then Samuel took the horn of oil and anointed him in the midst of his brothers; and the Spirit of the Lord came upon David from that day forward."*

That same Spirit rests on us today. And once the anointing comes upon your life, whether at birth, in youth, or in a later season, it changes everything. It sharpens your hearing. It strengthens your heart. And it confirms that what God has started in you, He will complete.

Conclusion:

From before I was born, God knew me. From the very foundation of the world, He had a plan. And that truth is not just about me, it's about you too. You are known. You are called. You are anointed. And when you embrace that, it truly becomes like fire shut up in your bones.

CHAPTER X

The Anointing Makes the Difference

Living Beyond Human Ability
Through the Power of the Spirit

"Then Samuel took the horn of oil and anointed him in the midst of his brothers; and the Spirit of the Lord came upon David from that day forward…" (1 Sam. 16:13).

Samuel went to the house of Jesse to anoint a king. Jesse brought his sons to the prophet one by one, but none of them were God's choice for king. Finally, Samuel asked Jesse if he had any other sons.

Jesse admitted that his youngest son, David, was out in the fields taking care of the sheep. When David was brought in from the fields to stand before the prophet, Samuel knew without a doubt that he was the one chosen by the Lord. Samuel anointed David with oil, consecrating him to the Lord's purpose.

From that moment forward, David's life was never the same. The Spirit of the Lord was on him from that day forward.

You see, **the anointing makes the difference**. It makes the difference between a boy practicing his slingshot alone in a field and a hero standing before a giant. It makes the difference between someone overlooked as a shepherd and that same person becoming a king ruling a nation.

And it doesn't stop with David. The anointing makes the difference in the church, in government, in business, in our schools, and in our homes. The anointing isn't just for ministers; it's for everyone who belongs to God.

Do You Realize the Difference?

Do you realize the difference the anointing can make in your life? The Spirit of God is ready to pour into you a level of anointing that will transform not only your calling but every area of your life. The Bible outlines different ways the anointing flows, and here are three that God is ready to release into your life:

1. Saturating Anointing

"It is like the precious oil upon the head, running down on the beard, the beard of Aaron, running down on the edge of his garments" (Ps. 133:2).

When Moses poured the anointing oil on Aaron's head, it flowed down Aaron's hair, past his beard, onto his clothes, and all the way down to his feet. Aaron wasn't just touched by the oil, he was drenched in it. He was saturated.

Today, we desperately need that kind of **saturating anointing**. Why? Because we aren't fighting small battles. We are facing cultural shifts, spiritual opposition, and personal struggles that are greater than anything previous generations could have imagined. A casual touch will not do. We need to be fully covered, drenched, and saturated in the power of God.

This kind of anointing equips us not just to survive, but to stand with authority, confidence, and courage. It's time to ask God to **saturate us in His Spirit** so that every word, every action, and every decision carries His presence.

2. Fresh Anointing

"…I have been anointed with fresh oil" (Ps. 92:10).

43

The truth is, we can grow stale. We can become routine in church, in ministry, even in our personal walk with God. What once felt vibrant can start to feel like an obligation. That's why we need a **fresh anointing.**

Ask yourself:

- Has church become a routine for me?
- Has my personal worship become a chore?
- Do I pray out of habit instead of hunger?

It doesn't have to stay that way. When the Holy Spirit brings a fresh anointing, everything changes. Worship feels alive again. Prayer feels powerful again. There's an energy, a quickening, and an atmosphere shift that you can't fake.

A fresh anointing brings back passion, restores boldness, and renews joy. It's like stepping into spring after a long winter; everything feels alive again.

3. Anointing of Wisdom and Favor

"But you have an anointing from the Holy One,
and you know all things" (1 John 2:20).

Another way the anointing works is by giving **wisdom and favor**. Wisdom allows you to make the right decisions at the right time. It gives clarity when confusion surrounds you, and it provides divine strategy when human logic falls short.

Favor, on the other hand, opens doors you could never open on your own. The Bible says, "For You, O Lord, will bless the righteous; with favor You will surround him as with a shield" (Ps. 5:12). When the anointing of favor is on your life, expect unexpected blessings. Opportunities will come your way. People will notice you. You will move from the back to the front, from overlooked to positioned.

Nothing Can Substitute the Anointing

The anointing makes all the difference. Nothing, and I mean nothing, can take its place.

We live in a world of substitutes. For every expensive name-brand item, there's a cheaper imitation. And while an imitation might fool someone for a moment, it never carries the same quality, value, or durability as the real thing.

In the same way, if we try to substitute charisma, intelligence, talent, or personality for the anointing of the Holy Spirit, we are deceiving ourselves. We might impress people for a short while, but only the anointing breaks yokes and sets people free. **Nothing can take the place of the anointing.**

What Happens When We Are Anointed

When we are anointed, it shows. It can't be hidden.

Acts 10:38 says, "...God anointed Jesus of Nazareth with the Holy Spirit and with power, who went about doing good and healing all who were oppressed by the devil, for God was with Him."

When Jesus was anointed, He didn't just keep it to Himself. He went out, and people's lives were changed. Healing came. Deliverance came. Hope came. The same is true for us.

When the anointing rests on your life:

- You begin to go about doing good.
- God opens doors you could never open on your own.
- Miracles, breakthroughs, and transformations begin to follow.

Press Into the Anointing

So, what do we do with this? The answer is simple: press in. Seek God with all your heart. Ask Him for a saturating anointing, for fresh anointing, and for wisdom and favor. Don't settle for what you had yesterday.

45

Keep coming back to Him again and again. The anointing isn't a one-time event; it's a continual flow from the Spirit of God.

Thank God we don't have to struggle with His work in our own limited power. We can walk in His Spirit. We can operate in His power. And truly, the **anointing makes all the difference**.

Chapter XI

THE ALL-SUFFICIENT WORD

The Foundation of Every Calling

There isn't any way that you can have a vibe to work for God through His calling without the infallible Word of God!! His Word must become your word.

A very dear mentor, Pastor Lindsey Croft, and his wife, who were viciously murdered by two drug addicts in their home, once told me something I have never forgotten: *"You will never go wrong as long as you preach JESUS."* Those words cut deep into my spirit. And really, how can you truly preach Jesus without knowing the Word of God?

The Word Is Perfect and Complete

Psalms 19:7-11 declares:

- **(7)** "The law of the LORD is perfect, converting the soul: the testimony of the LORD is sure, making wise the simple."

    This tells us the Bible is *perfect*. In fact, the Bible is the only revealed Truth in the world, and it always has been. It alone can "make wise the simple."

- **(8)** "The statutes of the LORD are right, rejoicing the heart: the commandment of the LORD is pure, enlightening the eyes."

  They are right not just because they come from the Lord, but because they are inherently and eternally right.

- **(9)** "The fear of the LORD is clean, enduring forever: the judgments of the LORD are true and righteous altogether."

  This is the kind of instruction that teaches us how to live with reverence toward God.

- **(10)** "More to be desired are they than gold, yea, than much fine gold: sweeter also than honey and the honeycomb."

  God's Word is worth more than riches. It is sweeter than the richest honey, far greater than any earthly treasure.

- **(11)** "Moreover by them is thy servant warned: and in keeping of them there is great reward."

  The Scriptures are not just information—they are a warning, an admonishment, and a promise of reward when obeyed.

One might say that Jesus dwelt in the Scriptures as the sun dwells in the heavens; the Scriptures both warned Him and sustained Him.

The Sufficiency of Scripture

I am talking about the **all-sufficiency of the Scripture.**

We are living in a day when the Word of God has been pin-knifed, stripped down by modernists and liberals. On the other hand, we're also in a time when preachers, even in evangelical circles, have diluted and weakened the Word of God. They have sabotaged it by refusing to believe in its inerrancy, by failing to take it as the sole authority for life and doctrine.

In other words, preaching has shifted from declaring that the Gospel *heals, delivers, and sets free* to a watered-down version that simply makes you *feel better.*

But I stand firm in saying "This": **The Scripture is sufficient for every human need.** There is no issue in life that cannot be addressed by this Book. If you need it, you will find it in the Word. If it is essential, you will discover the solution within its pages.

In this Book, we find the Wonderful Counselor, Jesus Christ Himself. He is the solution. He Himself is the personal answer for every human problem.

The Transforming Power of the Word

Psalm 19:7 reminds us:

> *"The law of the LORD is perfect, converting the soul: the testimony of the LORD is sure, making wise the simple."*

The Word transforms. "Perfect" means whole, complete, and sufficient. God's Word doesn't just inform, it converts the soul. It takes brokenness and makes it whole.

Too many people are striving and struggling to become something in their own effort. But the truth is this: anything you need from the Lord, you can receive through His Word.

- You cannot be **saved** without the Word. (1 Peter 1:23)
- You cannot be **sanctified** without the Word. (John 17:17)
- You cannot have the **Father without the Son**, and the Word makes this plain. (John 14:6)
- You cannot receive the **baptism of the Holy Spirit** without the Word. (Acts 10:44)
- You cannot experience **healing** apart from the Word. (Psalm 107:20)

Every great message is not man's idea but a proclamation of *"Thus saith the Word of God."*

God as the Rock in His Word

A pastor friend of mine lost nearly all his written materials in a fire. But the Word had been hidden in his heart, and that Word became a **Rock** he could stand on.

- "He is the Rock, His work is perfect..." (Deuteronomy 32:4)
- "Lead me to the Rock that is higher than I." (Psalm 61:2)
- "Upon this rock I will build My church; and the gates of hell shall not prevail against it." (Matthew 16:18)

The Rock is higher than any situation, stronger than any storm, and more unshakable than any opposition.

Even when the rains fall, the floods rise, and the winds blow, the house built on the Rock will stand (Matthew 7:24-25).

The Word as Refuge

The Word is not only a Rock, it is also a **Refuge.**

- "The LORD also will be a refuge for the oppressed, a refuge in times of trouble." (Psalm 9:9)
- "Thou art my hope in the day of evil." (Jeremiah 17:17)

When you are hidden in the Word, the enemy cannot find you.

God's Word is alive, potent, and powerful. I like to call it "Miracle-Grow High Octane." Isaiah 55:11 assures us that God's Word will not return void; it will accomplish the purpose for which it is sent.

The Word in Creation, the Word in Eternity

The Word of God is not new. It has always been, from before creation.

- *Before Creation:* "In the beginning was the Word, and the Word was with God, and the Word was God." (John 1:1)
- *Beginning of Creation:* "In the beginning God created the heaven and the earth." (Genesis 1:1)
- *Midst of Time:* "And the Word was made flesh and dwelt among us…" (John 1:14)
- *End of Time:* "…His name is called The Word of God." (Revelation 19:13)

From cradle to cross to crown—the Word has always been and always will be.

Living the Word

Here are my **Top 5 resolutions** for every Pastor, Preacher, Minister, Evangelist, Teacher, Prophet, and Saint:

1. **Study** – "Study to show thyself approved unto God…" (2 Timothy 2:15)
2. **Love** – "…the greatest of these is love." (1 Corinthians 13:13)
3. **Praise** – Praise and minister daily before the Lord. (2 Chronicles 8:13–15)
4. **Worship** – "For thou shalt worship no other god…" (Exodus 34:13)
5. **Pray** – "Pray without ceasing." (1 Thessalonians 5:17)

(Here's a simple structure: 5 minutes Thanksgiving, 5 minutes Repentance, 5 minutes Praying for God's Will, 5 minutes Rebuking the Devil, 5 minutes Praising.)

Are you praying every day? You should be, because prayer is where we both speak and listen to God. I call it question-and-answer time with the Lord.

Final Word

The all-sufficient Word of God is not just text on paper. It is life. It is power. It is the foundation of faith.

We must exercise our faith in God and His Word as we move ahead in this thing called life. And honestly, I don't know a better time than right now for each of us to recommit ourselves to Jesus Christ and His purpose.

Because all that we have talked about means nothing unless we mix it with faith.

Chapter XII

FAITH IS A SERIOUS THING!!

The Foundation of Faith

Hebrews 11:6 — *"But without faith it is impossible to please him: for he that cometh to God must believe that he is, and that he is a rewarder of them that diligently seek him."*

Two things concerning faith:

1. The Lord is the source of our faith. The moment you are born again, the Lord gives you a measure of faith.
2. This faith begins as a small seed, but it is designed to grow.

Romans 12:3 reminds us: *"For I say, through the grace given unto me, to every man that is among you, not to think of himself more highly than he ought to think; but to think soberly, according as God hath dealt to every man the measure of faith."*

From the very beginning, God has already planted within us the seed of faith. But like any seed, it requires nourishment, attention, and growth.

Faith Must Grow

We are not meant to stay at the starting point.

2 Thessalonians 1:3 says: *"We are bound to thank God always for you, brethren, as it is meet, because that your faith groweth exceedingly, and the charity of every one of you all toward each other aboundeth."*

Faith does grow, and it is our responsibility to develop it, as we allow the Word of God into our hearts. Just as a muscle becomes stronger with exercise, faith becomes powerful when exercised daily.

Ten Levels of Faith

1. Common Faith

Titus 1:4 — *"To Titus, mine own son after the common faith: Grace, mercy, and peace, from God the Father and the Lord Jesus Christ our Savior."*

As faith grows, it begins with **common faith**, that little seed. Jesus spoke of *faith as a grain of mustard seed.* The metaphor shows us that even the tiniest seed, when genuine, can produce powerful results.

- A mustard seed, though small, grows into a tree.
- Likewise, your faith, even if small at the beginning, has unlimited potential.
- Matthew 17:6 and Luke 17:6 emphasize that even mustard-seed faith can move mountains and uproot trees.

2. Weak Faith

Romans 4:19 — *"And being not weak in faith, he considered not his own body now dead, when he was about a hundred years old, neither yet the deadness of Sara's womb."*

This is **infant faith**-faith that struggles, wavers, and often limits God. It is common in new believers, but it is not meant to stay there.

3. Little Faith

Matthew 6:30 — *"Wherefore, if God so clothe the grass of the field, which to day is, and to morrow is cast into the oven, shall he not much more clothe you, O ye of little faith?"*

This is the faith that says *"if"*: *"Lord, if you want to do this, then maybe…"* It is hesitant faith that struggles with trust.

4. Temporary Faith

Luke 8:13 — *"They on the rock are they, which, when they hear, receive the word with joy; and these have no root, which for a while believe, and in time of temptation fall away."*

Faith that believes one day and doubts the next. This kind of faith fades under pressure.

5. Mental Faith / Active Faith

This is the faith that accepts the Lord and His promises, but it remains in the intellect and does not flow into power.

James 2:14-26 shows that faith must be accompanied by works. True faith becomes an **active force** that defeats all powers, even demonic ones.

6. Strong Faith

Romans 4:20 — *"He staggered not at the promise of God through unbelief; but was strong in faith, giving glory to God."*

This is Abraham's kind of faith-faith that refuses defeat and refuses to take *"no"* for an answer.

7. Great Faith

Matthew 8:10 — *"When Jesus heard it, he marveled, and said to them that followed, Verily I say unto you, I have not found so great faith, no, not in Israel."*

Great faith comes as the Word of God fills us. It is persistent and bold.

Matthew 15:28 adds: *"O woman, great is thy faith: be it unto thee even as thou wilt. And her daughter was made whole from that very hour."*

8. Unfeigned Faith

1 Timothy 1:5; 2 Timothy 1:5

This is faith that knows no hypocrisy. It is not loud or boastful—it is quiet, steady, powerful, and effective. It simply believes, and things happen.

9. Divine Faith

Galatians 2:20 — *"I am crucified with Christ: nevertheless I live; yet not I, but Christ liveth in me: and the life which I now live in the flesh I live by the faith of the Son of God, who loved me, and gave himself for me."*

This is the very faith of Christ Himself. It is filled with God's mighty power and brings answers to every prayer.

Faith Is in the Heart, Not the Mind

- Faith resides in the **heart** (the spirit).
- Hope is in the **mind** (the expectation).
- Faith moves forward—it has a destination.

Developed faith carries you from where you are to where God wants you to be.

What Developed Faith Brings

- **Full salvation** – Ephesians 2:8
- **Complete security** – 1 Peter 1:5

- **Answered prayer** – Mark 11:24
- **Healing** – James 5:14–15
- **An unshakable walk** – 2 Corinthians 5:7
- **Victory in daily life** – 1 John 5:4
- **A holy life** – Acts 15:9

As the Holy Spirit invades your life, this kind of faith begins to rise. It moves beyond human limits. **No earthly power can hinder this faith.**

Closing Thought:

Faith is no small matter. It is the very foundation of pleasing God, the seed that must grow, the force that moves us from weakness to strength, from common to divine. Faith is a serious thing because without it, we cannot see God's hand. With it, we walk in His promises and live in His victory.

Chapter XIII

YOUR FAITH MUST STAND TRIAL

The Call and the Challenge

I realize we have spent a considerable amount of time on subjects like the Word of God and now faith, but without a strong God-kind of faith, it is nearly impossible to trust that God has a call on your life and family.

The Christian walk and answering the call to ministry is a huge challenge when it all begins to unfold, and what is involved. There are, and there will be, battles to fight for your cause. Remember what David said to his brothers: *"Is there not a cause?"* Then he went out and killed Goliath. Thank God he had faith to go and wipe out the spiritual enemy.

If not yet, your faith **will be tried**, and in that trial, you will find out that God is right by your side. So, let's talk about your faith standing trial.

Abraham's Trial of Faith

Genesis 22:1-4, 9-12 tells the familiar story of Abraham:

> "And it came to pass after these things, that God did tempt Abraham, and said unto him,

Abraham: and he said, Behold, here I am. And he said, take now thy son, thine only son Isaac, whom thou lovest, and get thee into the land of Moriah; and offer him there for a burnt offering upon one of the mountains which I will tell thee of. And Abraham rose early in the morning, and saddled his ass, and took two of his young men with him, and Isaac his son, and clave the wood for the burnt offering, and rose, and went unto the place of which God had told him. Then on the third day Abraham lifted his eyes, and saw the place afar off... And they came to the place which God had told him of; and Abraham built an altar there, and laid the wood in order, and bound Isaac his son, and laid him on the altar upon the wood. And Abraham stretched forth his hand, and took the knife to slay his son. And the angel of the LORD called unto him out of heaven, and said, Abraham, Abraham: and he said, Here am I. And he said, Lay not thine hand upon the lad, neither do thou any thing unto him: for now I know that thou fearest God, seeing thou hast not withheld thy son, thine only son from me."

Abraham's trial proved his faith. And just like Abraham, our faith will be tested.

Why Faith Must Be Tried

1 Peter 1:7 reminds us: *"That the trial of your faith, being much more precious than of gold that perisheth, though it be tried with fire, might be found unto praise and honour and glory at the appearing of Jesus Christ."*
Your faith trial is worth more than money.

And 1 Peter 4:12 warns us: *"Beloved, think it not strange concerning the fiery trial which is to try you, as though some strange thing happened unto you."*

How many of you have felt strange in your trial? Yet the truth is, trials are not strange; they are expected.

The Reality of Our Times

Faith really needs to be understood and worked on! Faith is the engine that keeps our lives going.

We are living in perplexing and challenging times. The church struggles in ways unseen. We have raised a generation of people who cannot deal with delayed gratification. Everything must be now! Fast! Quick! Instead of us setting the pattern for the world, the world has set the pattern for us.

We have even peddled a gospel that was not gospel, making people think that God was Santa Claus, whose only function was to give gifts on demand. But faith does not exempt us from tragedy and adversity. Many have named it, claimed it, believed it, declared it, read all the material on faith, gone to all the workshops and seminars, and still faced persistent trouble.

Faith in the Furnace

Here is the unveiled truth: You will never know that you truly have faith until you are in a good fight.

Faith touches everything: family, workplace, health. People place their faith in alcohol, drugs, or worldly systems, while the believer places faith in God. The only real difference between a believer and a non-believer is this: one believes in God; the other believes in anything but God.

Could it be that your hard times are God's way of turning your eyes toward Him? Real faith is proven in the furnace of affliction. It shines not because you never went through anything, but because you did go through and held on to your integrity.

Stories of Faith

My daughter once told me several years ago that she had a church life but no story. Now she has a story of faith to tell.

That is the power of faith on trial: when the battle is over and you've got another notch in your belt, you also have a testimony that can help somebody else.

Hebrews 11 celebrates men and women of faith who endured trials, being sawn asunder, facing fiery darts, deserts, hunger, and more. Yet, despite it all, God saluted them for their faith.

The Church and the Call to Action

Sitting in the back row for nearly two years, I've watched the hurting come in and out of services without deliverance. I knew the church had the answer.

- Too many services end just when worship begins.
- Too many sermons are speeches that never declare healing and deliverance.
- Too many times, the sick are not prayed for, the hurting are not embraced, the broken are not told that God is in the house.

But **faith, family, and community** are critical to survival. By faith, healing still works today. By faith, the Holy Spirit still empowers. By faith, we must worship until His presence fills the room.

The Necessity of Trials

Sooner or later, your faith must stand trial. Whether single or married, rich or poor, young or old, you cannot escape the courtroom of God.

The saints of the ages faced death, crucifixion, beasts, and fire. What will our generation say? That someone gossiped about us? True faith is proven in greater battles than that.

Personal Testimony

I have been healed of leukemia, been through bankruptcy, and weathered rough times in marriage. And still, I am worth something to God. You are, too.

Think about what you've already endured. Every trial makes you worth more in God's eyes. If God trusted you with a battle, He trusted you because He knows you will come through.

Grace in the Fire

We often ask God to fix things He is not going to fix. Instead, He gives grace to stand. His strength is made perfect in weakness (2 Corinthians 12:9).

God becomes the thermostat in the furnace of affliction. He controls the heat. He tells the enemy, "Enough!" He equips you with peace that makes no sense to the world.

The Spirit Intercedes

When you couldn't pray for yourself, the Spirit prayed for you (Romans 8:26). He groaned for you through nights of depression and pain until breakthrough came. That is why you are still here. By the mercy of God, you live.

A Call to Praise

Let the redeemed of the Lord say so! You have a right to praise Him. If you survived the trial, you cannot keep silent. Tell your neighbor:

"I've got to praise Him!"

Because your survival is the evidence that **your faith has stood the trial**.

CHAPTER XIV

The Impact of the Holy Spirit on the Believer

A Message Close to My Heart

This is another one of my favorite messages that I want to share. Ephesians 1:15-21

> (15) Wherefore I also, after I heard of your faith in the Lord Jesus, and love unto all the saints, (16) Cease not to give thanks for you, making mention of you in my prayers; (17) That the God of our Lord Jesus Christ, the Father of glory, may give unto you the spirit of wisdom and revelation in the knowledge of him: (18) The eyes of your understanding being enlightened; that ye may know what is the hope of his calling, and what the riches of the glory of his inheritance in the saints, (19) And what is the exceeding greatness of his power to us-ward who believe, according to the working of his mighty power, (20) Which he wrought in Christ, when he raised him from the dead, and set him at his own right hand in the heavenly places, (21) Far above all principality, and power, and might, and dominion, and every

name that is named, not only in this world, but also in that which is to come.

Defining the Holy Spirit's Presence

Webster defines the Holy Spirit as *"the active presence of God in a human life."* Paul is addressing the church at Ephesus concerning their faith and wonderful position in Christ. He says, "Once I learned of your faithfulness, I do not cease to make mention of you in my prayers" (see vv. 15 & 16).

He points out the need for wisdom and a fresh revelation of the knowledge of Christ. Paul also discusses the power of the Holy Spirit in the life of the believer. In verses 18-21, Paul drives home the message of the "exceeding greatness of His power toward us who believe" (NKJV).

We have been given the power to represent Him in the world. We have been given authority to go in His name.

The Goal of Salvation

*****My GOAL is to get every single person Saved first… The challenge is getting every person to realize they need a Savior or a life change.

Saved means:

- **Love God with all your heart.**

  Deuteronomy 11:13 – *And it shall come to pass, if ye shall hearken diligently unto my commandments which I command you this day, to love the LORD your God, and to serve him with all your heart and with all your soul.*

- **To be Obedient.**

  1 Samuel 15:22 – *Hath the LORD as great delight in burnt offerings and sacrifices, as in obeying the voice of the LORD? Behold, to obey is better than sacrifice, and to hearken than the fat of rams.*

- **To Trust in the Lord.**

   Proverbs 3:5 – *Trust in the LORD with all thine heart; and lean not unto thine own understanding.*

- **I will Praise and Worship God.**

   2 Corinthians 11:12 – *But what I do, that I will do, that I may cut off occasion from them which desire occasion; that wherein they glory, they may be found even as we.*

The Believer Is Filled With Power

Once a person becomes a believer, then power comes from on high. Meaning we can then receive the gift of the Holy Spirit.

- **His power is poured out upon us.**

   Luke 24:49 – *And, behold, I send the promise of my Father upon you: but tarry ye in the city of Jerusalem, until ye be endued with power from on high.* Acts 1:8 – *But ye shall receive power, after that the Holy Ghost is come upon you: and ye shall be witnesses unto me both in Jerusalem, and in all Judaea, and in Samaria, and unto the uttermost part of the earth.*

- **His abiding power helps us.**

   John 14:16 – *And I will pray the Father, and he shall give you another Comforter, that he may abide with you for ever.*

- **He dwells in us in power.**

   John 14:17 – *Even the Spirit of truth, whom the world cannot receive, because it seeth him not, neither knoweth him: but ye know him; for he dwelleth with you, and shall be in you.*

Baptized in the Holy Spirit and Fire

Matthew 3:11 – *I indeed baptize you with water unto repentance: but he that cometh after me is mightier than I, whose shoes I am not worthy to bear: he shall baptize you with the Holy Ghost, and with fire.*

🔥 Fire is a powerful force that can energize and purify us. Fire can power a locomotive or propel a spacecraft to the moon. The fire of the Spirit catches the attention of the believer and unbeliever alike and can propel the Church today.

The Believer Receives Boldness

- During the Passion Week, Peter cowardly denied Christ. But on the Day of Pentecost, he was transformed into a bold preacher (Acts 2:14-41).
- No matter how bad you think you are, God can make you into a person that He can use.

The spirit of fear has been conquered.

2 Timothy 1:7 – *For God hath not given us the spirit of fear, but of power, and of love, and of a sound mind.*

Three thousand people were saved and added to the church in one day. After the healing of the lame man and being commanded to stop preaching in the name of Jesus, Peter prays for *"all boldness"* to speak the Word of God:

Acts 4:29-31 – *And now, Lord, behold their threatening: and grant unto thy servants, that with all boldness they may speak thy word, by stretching forth hand to heal; and that signs and wonders may be done by the name of thy holy child Jesus. And when they had prayed, the place was shaken where they were assembled together; and they were all filled with the Holy Ghost, and they spake the word of God with boldness.*

Witnessing More Effectively

The Holy Spirit is sent by the Father to help us.

John 14:26 – *But the Comforter, which is the Holy Ghost, whom the Father will send in my name, he shall teach you all things, and bring all things to your remembrance, whatsoever I have said unto you.*

He teaches us all things. He reminds us of all things that we need to say and do. He prompts us by the leading of the Spirit. Out of nowhere, our hopes and motives just change for the better.

As we listen for the voice of the Spirit, we hear the Spirit of truth.

John 14:17 – *Even the Spirit of truth, whom the world cannot receive, because it seeth him not, neither knoweth him: but ye know him; for he dwelleth with you, and shall be in you.*

We Are Completed to Praise God

The multitudes in Jerusalem heard them praising God.

Acts 2:6 – *Now when this was noised abroad, the multitude came together, and were confounded, because that every man heard them speak in his own language.*

Acts 2:11 – *Cretes and Arabians, we do hear them speak in our tongues the wonderful works of God.*

They said, *"We hear them declaring the wonders of God in our own tongues!"* (v. 11 NIV).

They spoke in languages unknown to themselves, but known to the people hearing them. The Church was unified, and together they praised the Lord daily (Acts 2:40-47).

They had favor with all the people because of their joyous testimonies of praise. *"For praise from the upright is beautiful"* (Psalm 33:1 NKJV).

The Great Impact of the Holy Spirit

The great impact of the Holy Spirit on the believer was this: *"And great grace was upon them all."* (Acts 4:33).

Would you like for Great Grace to be on you too???

CHAPTER XV

THE NECESSITY OF THE HOLY SPIRIT IN YOUR LIFE

Sealed by the Power of the Spirit with God in Our Midst

II Corinthians 4:8–9

> "(8) We are troubled on every side, yet not distressed; we are perplexed, but not in despair;
>
> (9) Persecuted, but not forsaken; cast down, but not destroyed."

As we look back over time, it appears we have tried as many ways as we can to devastate the gifts God has given us. Biologists say we are smothering plant life with over-proliferation and overconsumption. Physicists say we are degenerating human life through radiation and pollution. Biochemists say we are suffering a brain drain because of drug abuse and insufficient educational opportunities. Sociologists say rip-off and greed are accepted norms. Theologians ask, *"Whatever happened to the meaning of sin, and where have Judeo-Christian moral values gone?"*

Yet, the Bible comes crashing through with a pattern for living that provides the ability to cope regardless of circumstances. God's people may be down, but they are never out!

So many Christians have been down in times past. But it's time to get up. There's a miracle inside of you that won't die… Give that miracle away. This is the message of:

II Corinthians 4:8–9

"We are hard pressed on every side, yet not crushed; we are perplexed, but not in despair; persecuted, but not forsaken; struck down, but not destroyed."

This is a new day, and we're living the vision that God has given us.

A New Dimension of Vision

A new dimension to that vision is this: *Reach out—do something that you have never done before.*

The devil suckered believers out of the church; now we're going to sucker them back in.

We have reached out to the world long enough for answers: to the world, to other churches, to our own opinions. Now we must reach out to something greater, to intensify our faith.

- **God** – 1 John 4:4
  "Ye are of God, little children, and have overcome them: because greater is he that is in you, than he that is in the world."

- **Word** – Hebrews 4:12
  "For the word of God is quick, and powerful, and sharper than any two-edged sword, piercing even to the dividing asunder of soul and spirit, and of the joints and marrow, and is a discerner of the thoughts and intents of the heart."

- **Worship** – John 4:24
    "God is a Spirit: and they that worship him must worship him in spirit and in truth."

- **Community** – Matthew 9:37
    "Then saith he unto his disciples, The harvest truly is plenteous, but the laborers are few."

When It Looks Like Satan Is Winning

So often, we feel that as believers, we are losing. Sometimes it may seem like Satan is winning, but God always provides a way out for His own.

- When Adam and Eve were sent from the Garden of Eden because they had sinned, it looked like Satan was winning... **but God raised up Noah.**
- When the people turned from God and began building the Tower of Babel, it looked like Satan was winning... **but God raised up Abraham.**
- When Israel was in Egypt's bondage, it looked like Satan was winning... **but God raised up Moses.**
- When God's people built a golden calf at Mount Sinai, it looked like Satan was winning... **but God raised up Joshua.**
- When Israel was in Babylonian captivity, it looked like Satan was winning... **but God raised up Daniel.**
- When God was silent for 400 years, it looked like Satan was winning... **but God raised up His Son, Jesus Christ.**
- When Christ died on the cross, it looked like Satan was winning... **but God sent the power of the Holy Spirit.**

Sealed by the Spirit

The only way we can survive is by the power of the Spirit in us that sustains and renews us. **He seals us.**

- **This seal provides access to the Father**
  Ephesians 1:13 – "In whom ye also trusted, after that ye heard the word of truth, the gospel of your salvation: in whom also after that ye believed, ye were sealed with that Holy Spirit of promise." Ephesians 2:18 – "For through him we both have access by one Spirit unto the Father."

The devil doesn't have the access that you have. You need the Holy Ghost.

- **This seal strengthens our inner being**
  Ephesians 3:16 – "That he would grant you, according to the riches of his glory, to be strengthened with might by his Spirit in the inner man."

- **This seal gives us unity and peace**
  Ephesians 4:4 – "There is one body, and one Spirit, even as ye are called in one hope of your calling."

- **This seal fills us**
  Ephesians 5:18 – "And be not drunk with wine, wherein is excess; but be filled with the Spirit."

Living by His Spirit

We need to learn to live by His Spirit regardless.
The Spirit motivated Christ.
The Spirit brought Jesus into the world,
anointed Him, baptized Him, and filled Him.

The Spirit took Him to Calvary, placed Him at the Father's right hand, and gave Him the intercessory work.

Galatians 5:16 – "This I say then, Walk in the Spirit, and ye shall not fulfil the lust of the flesh."

When we understand this, we begin to understand what the renewed life is all about: *If any man be in Christ...*

We begin to see what God wants to do in our lives. Are you beginning to see what God wants to do in your life?

The greatest untapped source of power in the world is the **Power of the Holy Spirit**. And that power is available to renew each life.

Let your anointing live. Let your miracle go forth. Be filled with His Spirit.

Chapter XVI

ALWAYS ON GUARD!!

A Call to Vigilance

> "...Abstain from pollutions of idols, and from fornication...."
>
> — *Acts 15:20*

We must never forget that the devil is always on the prowl, waiting for us to drop our guard and fall asleep on the job so he can stealthily find an entrance into our lives. In our moments of lethargy and complacency, we are especially vulnerable.

The enemy is constantly poised to exploit any perceivable weakness, and when he makes his move, it is often with devastating consequences. Therefore, we must perpetually remain on guard, diligent, wide-awake, and doing our part to protect ourselves from the evil lurking in the shadows.

Avoiding Spiritually Negative Environments

Specifically, this means we must be vigilant about not exposing ourselves to environments that have spiritually negative consequences. An integral part of being vigilant is to stay away from places, events, and people that are detrimental to our spiritual lives.

The Bible makes it clear that it is our duty to avoid anything that is opposed to a life of holiness. By doing so, we fulfill our part in protecting ourselves from the evil in the world. This is our responsibility, and God expects us to fulfill it seriously.

Much like today, the early Church was literally surrounded on all sides by things that could easily lure new believers back into a life of sin. The spiritual leadership in Jerusalem made the decision, under the inspiration of the Holy Spirit, that we all need to be careful about the places, events, and people we allow in our lives.

Watch Out for Dream Killers

There's a wake-up call for you to be more vigilant about where you go, what you do, and whom you spend time with. Especially watch out for **DREAM KILLERS.**

I had to learn the hard way about telling my hopes and aspirations to non-dreamers because they will stop you in your tracks with their negativity. They cannot see what God has placed in your spirit, and they will attempt to pull you down to the level of their unbelief.

If nothing else, let the Holy Spirit speak to you about walking in greater spiritual freedom and holiness.

Creating Safe Distance

My friend, there are places, events, and people that are spiritually detrimental to your future. Rather than put yourself in jeopardy by allowing these things in your life, it is safer to put distance between them and yourself.

Since the devil is on the prowl, it is essential always to remain on guard, diligent, wide-awake, and doing our part to protect ourselves from the evil that is in the world. This means putting distance between ourselves and any individual, activity, or atmosphere that could contribute to our spiritual demise.

A Final Challenge

So I ask you today: **Are you sensibly putting space between yourself and detrimental places, events, and people that aren't healthy for you?**

That was God's requirement 2,000 years ago, and it is still what the Holy Spirit requires of you today!

CHAPTER XVII

Training Yourself to Hear God Speak

Hearing God Speak

I have seen God do some Amazing things. I have also seen men mess up some Amazing things as well!! Without a doubt, it is only the Holy Spirit that can speak to you from the Father. He said, *"I will only speak what I heard the Father say."*

You cannot hear God calling you and imparting special gifts without the power of the Holy Spirit.

God's Instruction Manual

John 16:13 says: *"Howbeit when he, the Spirit of truth, is come, he will guide you into all truth: for he shall not speak of himself; but whatsoever he shall hear, that shall he speak: and he will shew you things to come."*

I have truly spent a lot of time sitting in services, on the front porch, lying awake at all hours of the night. Currently, it is 3:50 a.m., and I know that I feel and hear the Holy Spirit speaking to me about where I've been and maybe even a direction forward.

A Pastor's Encouragement

In 1999, I was teaching a series on Salvation when a very special pastor friend stopped by our Sunday evening service. He asked me where I got the material that I was teaching. I explained that I was intrigued by the verse 2 Corinthians 5:17 and began a study on it:

> *"Therefore if any man be in Christ, he is a new creature; old things are passed away; behold, all things are become new."*

He said that it was a great and powerful teaching and that I should write a book. Well, you remember earlier we discussed the fact that God will give you a new name in your calling/anointing. So I took it to heart and did the research, and made notes like a sermon to preach.

From Notes to Anointed Words

What I found out was that as I talked about what was in the notes through preaching, it became anointed preaching—preaching under the unction of the Holy Spirit. When I had the preaching tapes transcribed and read through them, I found that I was reading an anointed story.

There were many deep things that were said that were not in the notes. So through several years, I ended up with five books published, one ready to publish (*Lucifer Did Me a Favor*), and working on this project, which will hopefully help one to identify their calling.

To say that I have been sad about closing the church doors and having all of these books in storage would be an understatement.

God's Call Still Remains

As I am writing this story through many heartfelt tears, I am so grateful that God's call is still there and that He still has work to be completed. I have this publisher in another state that continues to bombard me with calls about my books. They said if I updated and made a few changes, they could get my writings worldwide.

Therefore, I felt like rereading the books again to refresh what I had written. Before, I did research to have a sermon. Now, I read just because I want to refresh the subjects.

A Light Came On

Now, in reading, I realized all the years I was seeking somebody's material that I could help my people be strong in their faith. I mean, endlessly searching for answers. I never could really land material that would be lasting and permanently impactful.

As I began to read each book, by the third one, it was like a light came on!! Not even realizing how one book tied into the next and so on. I thought, *My Lord, God had given me the guide on how to raise up a strong believer right before my eyes.*

A Blueprint in the Books

- One book dealt with **Salvation**
- The next, **Understanding the Spiritual Enemy**
- Then, **Praise and Worship**
- To the **7 times Christ bled**
- To the **Poisons that find their way into our lives**
- To **What Heaven will be like**
- And number seven: **Discovering The Life You Were Created For !**

We had changed the name of the church five times, trying to find the right name, when God had given me the name before we ever started the church, but I thought it was too strong: **Intensive Care Ministries.**

Rethinking Growth

In reviewing the books, I realized what I/we had done. We would plow and look for the harvest by numerical growth. But that isn't what the Word teaches.

1 Corinthians 3:6-7: *"I have planted, Apollos watered; but God gave the increase. So then neither is he who plants anything, neither he who waters; but God gave the increase."*

Man, in his own ability, cannot bring about the increase, no matter how much he plants or waters, spiritually speaking, that's God's part.

We stayed busy plowing, planting, watering, fertilizing, building programs, and looking for the increase. And that, my friend, is not the way it's supposed to be.

The Real Work

We should have been teaching the material that God gave through my books, through His anointing, and of course, become students of God's Holy Word. It's not that plowing, planting, and watering were a bad idea, but so often we had conditioned the people to major on special projects, which became almost like the main thing.

The last year before the big change, the congregation gave over one hundred thousand dollars to special projects. We were busy celebrating all that had been accomplished with our hands.

Again, all the special works were not bad; it's just that we never took time to dig DEEP into a subject such as being *In Christ, not of Christ.*

Life-Altering Subjects

All of the writings that God gave us, like a blueprint, were on life-altering subjects. So it truly is okay that we took this journey for nearly 25 years.

We did experience hundreds being saved and many healed of sickness, others filled with the baptism of the Holy Spirit, others getting involved with ministry and major missions projects.

We just didn't understand that we needed to go deep into the blueprint that God gave us. And for myself and family, some sabbaticals along the way would have been life-giving.

A Time of Refreshing

This over three-year sabbatical that I have been on has been like the old, old chorus: *"He washed my eyes with tears that I could clearly see!"* Just taste and see that the Lord is good. These subjects are life-changing through the anointing of God.

A Glimpse at the Books

- **Salvation: It's Not What I Thought It Was** – More than a prayer in your head; it's a birth in your heart. Salvation is the beginning, not the end, of the story. Becoming like Christ is a lifelong journey.
- **Souls Under Siege** – Countless souls who come to the altar in a time of emotional conviction are often too soon lost to the church, and harder to win back than if they had never come.
- **Don't Let the Rocks Cry Out** – Longing for intimacy with the Lord? Rigid tradition replaced by living praise and worship.
- **His Pain, My Gain** – His blood is about more than just the Easter story. It is the doorway to deeper power in our spiritual journey.
- **Poison in the Pot** – Identifying hidden poisons in our lives that can spiritually destroy us.
- **Lucifer Did Me a Favor** – A surprising perspective on spiritual warfare that inspires our walk with God and builds excitement for Heaven.

CHAPTER XVIII

WE ARE FREE TO MOVE AHEAD

A Call to Action

This is another one of my favorite messages that I wanted to share in this writing. We are free to move ahead. This message is direct to one's soul. Your calling always calls for action. This message speaks on the need to respond in the world in which you live to respond to what you feel in your heart towards God's calling.

Matthew 11:12 *And from the days of John the Baptist until now the kingdom of heaven suffereth violence, and the violent take it by force.*

I believe God has ordered this time for you. You must believe God orders special times for you to get involved. That's His business, to order just what you need. We are moving as a people and as the family of God, not only just here but worldwide. God is doing some things.

Do you understand that God is alive and well? God is moving His people; He's pulling them together to become one powerful force in this world. We're moving toward the greatest move of God that the earth has ever witnessed. If you're not ready to move with God, you'll be left behind.

The real secret to success is this: **Find out what God is saying about something, what God feels about it, what God directs about it, and then follow through with it.**

The Battlefield of the Mind

We are the army of God, and we are to go against what comes against God's plan. We are an army for God against Satan, against the evil in this world.

Satan would like us to be in:

- Romans 1:28 — with a reprobate mind.
- Ephesians 4:17 — with a fuddled mind.
- Colossians 2:18 — with a puffed-up mind.
- Romans 8:7 — with a carnal mind.
- Titus 1:15 — with a defiled mind.

But God calls us to:

- Romans 8:6 — to have a spiritual mind.
- Romans 12:2 — to have a transformed mind.
- 1 Corinthians 2:16 — to have a mind like Christ.
- Ephesians 4:23 — to have a renewed mind in Him.
- 2 Timothy 1:7 — to have a sound mind.

Taking Ground for God

We are to take ground for God. That's our mission today, to take ground for God. To do that, you're going to have to take it away from the devil. What God doesn't possess, the devil does.

We are ambassadors commissioned by God in the earth to subdue the earth, to take away what Satan has captured and give it back to God. It's a wonderful job, but it will take an army of committed people.

Not only are we to possess new ground, but sometimes we need to go back and recapture old ground that was stolen. **If you've lost some ground for God, boldly go back and recover it.** God will give you power and wisdom through His Spirit to recover lost ground.

Occupying the Land

God doesn't have a place in the Bible where He tells you to lose it all. We are also to occupy the land we're already in.

Occupy is a military term meaning *get in there, take over, stay in there, and be in charge.* Let the devil and the community know that you are here to stay.

- Go for new ground.
- Recover old ground.
- Build and keep what you've got.

The Power of Prophecy

We have the keys to the Kingdom of Heaven—prophecy the vision instead of telling your business.

You must learn how to prophesy.

When you are praying and God begins to show you what He wants, you've got to get it out of your spirit by prophesying. You must begin to declare it. You must begin to speak those words.

Mark 11:23 *For verily I say unto you, Whosoever shall say unto this mountain, Be thou removed, and be thou cast into the sea; and shall not doubt in his heart, but shall believe that those things which he saith shall come to pass; he shall have whatsoever he saith.*

This is what I'm saying: **I declare that the glory of God be here, miracles flow, lives be saved, and multitudes stream here to receive and to become part of this great opportunity to experience God's goodness.**

A New Thing

God has made us to be free. He's got a plan for you. We must move to some new areas today.

Isaiah 43:18 *Remember ye not the former things, neither consider the things of old.*

Isaiah 43:19 *Behold, I will do a new thing; now it shall spring forth; shall ye not know it? I will even make a way in the wilderness, and rivers in the desert.*

God hasn't told us everything there is yet. Tradition repeats the same old thing, but God is saying: "I am going to do something new." It's an age of revelation. It's a time of praise and worship. It's a season of servanthood where people care more for others than for themselves.

We are free to serve!

Trends God Is Using in the Church Today

- Worship — God is moving through the worship of His people.
- Attendance — Large churches are growing, but God is also working powerfully in small gatherings.
- Worldwide Revival — Today, million of Spirit-filled believers are impacting the world.
- The Church United — Unity is releasing great works, just like in the Upper Room.

Living in Freedom

Six facts to remember concerning being free to answer the call of God in your life:

1. Free from sin. (1 Peter 2:24)
2. Free from sickness. (Matthew 8:17)
3. Free from needs and lack. (Philippians 4:19)
4. Free from demonic power. (Luke 10:19)
5. Free to worship and praise. (Isaiah 43:21; Isaiah 61:11)
6. Free to do great works for God. (John 14:12)

A Personal Confirmation

Here's another confirmation of God's calling—
Dr. Tom Frye writes about Pastor Don R. Vining:

"You are a man who has devoted his life to faith, family, and community. You have lived in the same area with your devoted wife, raised your children, and now delight in your grandchildren. Known for your kindness and humor, you give when it's easy, and you give when the cost is great. You have reached out with a healing hand to care for hurting people, not only in your community but beyond. And through the years, no matter the challenge, you have remained steadfast in your call to minister. Whether it meant selling watermelons by the roadside, tractors to farmers, or standing alone, you were determined to keep going. The life of Don R. Vining reminds me of the words from Galatians 6:9: *'Let us not become weary in doing good, for at the proper time we will reap a harvest if we do not give up.'* It is my honor to say of Don R. Vining — a faithful servant, a determined minister, and a man whose life speaks louder than words."

CHAPTER XIX

THE WORDS KEEP COMING!

When You Think It's Finished...

I told my wife a couple of nights ago that I had finished this writing, but here I go again with more to say. I'm reminded of the pastor who kept saying he was trying to dismiss the Sunday service, but he felt someone needed to obey the Lord and speak what God was saying to them!

A Word From a Friend

A pastor friend of mine contacted me, and as I told him what I was feeling about this project and future ministry involvement, he interrupted me and said, *I knew all along that you weren't finished and you would be back stronger than before.*

He said, *That's why I never stopped praying for you!* He said, *Don Vining, you are a part of the remnant that God will use in an end-time Revival.*

He went on to say:

- God is going to use people who know what **pain** is, what it means to be **broken**, and how to **recover**.
- He told me I had encouraged him without even realizing how broken and sad he was at times.

- He reminded me that God gave me the ability to just talk and let the chips fall where they will.
- And that when I don't know what to say, the Holy Spirit will fill my mouth with **Rivers of Living Water** that spring forth healing.

He concluded, *Only the once broken can be used in that manner.*

Speaking From Experience

I think back through the years growing up in church, and I don't remember the pastors ever talking about their personal battles. Yes, we did get the Word, but not many personal battles.

I think this is where I may have stayed in trouble, using lived-out battles tied with the Word of God and His power to bring you through to victory.

A few years back, my family had been going through a gut-wrenching heartbreak, and as I shared about the pain, one of the men in our congregation said that he would not be back because he did not come to church to hear about my problems but wanted to hear the Word of God.

I thought that was so interesting because the entire church for the past two years walked with this same family while his grandson was awaiting a kidney transplant. Literally every service we gave updates and devoted much prayer time to this matter. Even when the call came that there was a donor and the surgery would take place within hours, I left our family vacation and drove over two hours home to be with this family.

I thought it was amazing that it was okay to talk about their issues but not about mine.

End-Time Ministry and the Broken

I believe that the successful end-time ministries will be the ones that get **down deep in the ditch with the broken.** It's because we speak out of the experience of being crushed.

87

Recently, I sat in a church with about 200 in attendance, listening to the pastor seemingly read a sermon. Suddenly, he stepped away from his notes and began to spill out where he had come from.

He talked about:

- Troubles he had experienced in a church where he once led worship.
- The pain of going through an ugly divorce while serving in ministry.
- The feeling of being under-valued and unqualified to help others when he couldn't keep his own family together.

That day, his raw honesty and humility brought me to tears. That was probably the most profound message I had experienced in that church, just raw, down-in-the-ditch truth from the ashes of ruin.

Who God Is Looking For

I want to say that God isn't looking for someone who has it all together. He's looking for the bruised, the battered, and the beaten low.

Have you ever heard the phrase *"out of the ashes of ruin"*? The devil may be telling you that you can't possibly be used by God. But I want to proclaim: **you are exactly who God is looking for.**

All of those broken times are there as a platform for you to identify, or be reminded of, the fact that **you are still the one God needs.**

Out of all the brothers, you may just be the little insignificant David out on the back pastures tending the sheep... but soon you will rise and declare: **IS THERE NOT A CAUSE!**

A Test of Alignment

I wanted to confirm this writing by my own life, to be sure my thinking is in line with what's being said.

Therefore, I petitioned another one of my pastor friends with the same question as before: *If you were going to rename Don R. Vining with a biblical name based on what you knew of my ministry and family, what would it be?*

This was his answer:

> Pastor Josh Saramento said—
> *"The rebranding should reflect Legacy, Strength, Vision, and Faithfulness. You have been a builder of people, churches, and even families, while being a patriot, a man of the Word, and a stern-but-loving shepherd. The biblical identity could bring together those qualities. Pastor Vining—The Kingdom Builder. Builder—Nehemiah/Paul identity. Kingdom—his patriotism, family values, and faith united. Legacy—husband, father, grandfather. 'Building Churches. Building Families. Building Futures.'"*

God Uses the Broken

God is calling people who aren't afraid to talk about being crushed and broken!

When you see yourself as nothing, you never really know what others see in you. But may you allow the Spirit of God to lead, guide, and direct your path.

Always remember: He knew of you before the foundation of the world was formed. And He wants to use whoever is willing!

CHAPTER XX

HE'S STILL GOD!!

When Pain Clouds Your Calling

I know when you are hurt, especially in your calling, it at times feels like God checked out. But I want to emphasize the importance of looking past your pain and feelings to the fact that by faith, God is still near, and most of all, He is STILL GOD. No matter what!

Recently, I watched a UFC fight where the two fighters beat each other until you couldn't even recognize them for all the blood. It was almost sickening to watch. The truth of the matter is that at times we go through seemingly bloody fights on behalf of our calling.

Faith in the Midst of Tragedy

Recently, there was a church where students had gathered to pray over the new school year when a shooter fired through the windows. Two children died, many were injured, and the shooter then took his own life, leaving behind hate notes.

A little boy later told how his friend pushed him to the floor and lay on top of him to protect him. That friend was one of the wounded. Publicly, the boy gave thanks for his friend and for God's protection. But the very next day, swelling appeared in his own neck, and doctors found a bullet fragment lodged right next to his carotid artery.

How many times have we come so very close to spiritual death, which is the devil's aim, to take you out? It is easy at times to feel like you are all alone, but then the Bible comes crashing through with Hebrews 11 and the great cloud of witnesses.

I want to punch every reader in their spiritual gut and say: **RUN ON. DON'T GET WEARY.**

Faith Must Stand Trial

We've already talked about the fact that your faith must stand trial. Many times, just when you are about to get the breakthrough, that's when temptation comes to cause you to faint and become exasperated.

But hear me — **you'll win if you don't quit.**

One preacher said, *"Run on, don't be weary."* Another declared, *"If you're afraid, then go afraid!"*

When Life Knocks You Down

Many years ago, on Thanksgiving Eve, my wife and I were out for a motorcycle ride when suddenly the car in front of us stopped at a light. I was sightseeing, and my wife yelled for me to STOP. We hit the car and went down. The handlebar cut into me, and as I lay in excruciating pain, my wife yelled again: *"Get up out of the road before you get run over!"*

I remember saying, *"I'm hurting and I can't move."* She yelled again: *"GET UP!"* Somehow, strength came from nowhere, and I got up and moved out of the road.

I know what it feels like to be sucker-punched in the gut and unable to move. But you must find the strength to **GET UP and run on into your calling.**

The Call That Won't Go Away

For months, I was upset with a pastor friend who kept telling me, *"You've got to get up and move beyond the moment."* I didn't want to hear it. I blocked him out.

But since the day we closed the church, the publishers have been that same relentless voice I could not escape. No matter how many times I rejected them, they just kept coming. One lady, who didn't even know me, argued with me: *"Pastor, you can't put all these experiences in writing and just leave them in the attic. The world needs to hear what you've got to say."*

She kept calling, begging, pleading. And I couldn't even talk to my own family about the possibility because of all the pain they had been through.

Believe me, as I write this, I am crying and hearing God's voice speaking to me as well. If you really knew me, you would know I am anything but a crybaby. This writing could very well be God's constant call for you, too, to **get up and run on!**

Run With Endurance

Hebrews 12:1 reminds us: *"Wherefore seeing we also are compassed about with so great a cloud of witnesses, let us lay aside every weight, and the sin which doth so easily beset us, and let us run with patience the race that is set before us."*

Verse 2 continues: *"Looking unto Jesus the author and finisher of our faith; who for the joy set before him endured the cross…"*

What was that joy? Beatings, scourging, cursing, bleeding seven times, hanging on a cross, buried in a borrowed tomb? Could it mean that we, too, should face hardship with the **joy of the Lord** as our strength?

Verse 3 exhorts: *"Consider him that endured such contradiction of sinners against himself, lest ye be wearied and faint in your minds."*

So I ask you again: **Do you have any faith?**

The Question of Faith

Hebrews 11:6 says: *"But without faith it is impossible to please Him…"*

There are all kinds of faith — Common Faith, Weak Faith, Little Faith, Temporary Faith, Mental Faith, Active Faith, Strong

Faith, Great Faith, and even times when it seems like there is **no faith at all.**

But here is the real question: Do you have faith in what you face right now?

When your entire world blows up in your face, when it's no longer somebody else's crisis but your own, **do you still have faith?**

Prophesy to Yourself

As believers, I want us to learn to prophesy to ourselves:

- #ViningStrong
- #FaithStrong
- #WordStrong
- #JehovahStrong
- #DeterminedStrong
- #HolyGhostStrong
- #DevilKickingStrong
- #OvercomingStrong
- #PraisingStrong

Declare with your own mouth: *"Devil, I have the joy, strength, and power of the Lord!"*

You may feel betrayed like Joseph, lied on at Potiphar's house, incarcerated wrongly, or broke down to your last dime. But don't count yourself out, because God is still God, and you will rise again!

The Great Cloud of Witnesses

On the basis of Hebrews 11, we know that all those heroes made it: Abel, Enoch, Noah, Sarah, Abraham, Gideon, Rahab, and more. They didn't have cars, TVs, Bibles, support groups, or counseling. Yet THEY MADE IT.

Now they fill the grandstands of Heaven, watching you run your race, cheering you on: *"Don't quit. Run on!"*

Somebody's watching you. Somebody's praying for you. Somebody's encouraging you. Somebody's standing up for you. Don't you dare stop now.

Don't Live in the Past

Remember Samuel mourning for Saul? God had to tell him in 1 Samuel 16:1: *"How long will you mourn for Saul? Fill your horn with oil and go..."*

In other words: stop looking back. Stop longing for yesterday. Don't be like Lot's wife. God has new oil, new anointing, new direction.

Dwelling in the Secret Place

Psalms 91:1 declares: *"He that dwelleth in the secret place of the Most High shall abide under the shadow of the Almighty."*

It's time to step into that secret place. Time to get your "secret" — a fresh divine word.

Final Reminder

Most of all, remember this one truth that cannot be shaken: **God is still God!!**

Chapter XXI

A Summary Chapter to Discovering The Life You Were Created For !

Identifying a call from God involves seeking Him through prayer, studying scripture, and discerning the specific ways He is leading you. It also means paying attention to your passions, talents, and how you feel when exploring different paths, as well as seeking guidance from trusted mentors.

1. Seek God's Presence and Guidance

Prayer

Start by praying for clarity and direction, asking God to reveal His will for your life. Calling is not about rushing into action but about first waiting on Him. Prayer opens your spirit to hear what the Father is saying.

Study Scripture

Regularly immerse yourself in God's Word. His Word is a lamp unto your feet and a light unto your path (Psalm 119:105). Scripture provides both timeless principles and living guidance. The stories of Moses, Gideon, Esther, and Paul remind us that God calls ordinary people to extraordinary assignments.

Listen to the Holy Spirit

Pay attention to those moments when you feel a strong prompting or conviction. The Holy Spirit often speaks with a quiet nudge or deep inner assurance. Remember, the Spirit will never lead you in contradiction to God's Word or His character.

2. Reflect on Your Passions and Talents

Identify Your Passions

What activities do you genuinely enjoy and feel drawn to? God often places desire in our hearts as a signpost toward our purpose (Psalm 37:4).

Recognize Your Talents

What are you naturally good at? What gifts, skills, and abilities has God given you that bring joy and fruit when used? Every believer has been given spiritual gifts for the building up of the body (1 Corinthians 12:4-7).

Consider Your Personality

How does your personality type influence how you might best serve God? Some are called to lead from the front, while others serve faithfully behind the scenes. Both are essential in the kingdom.

3. Seek Wise Counsel

Talk to Trusted Mentors

Share your thoughts and feelings with those who walk closely with God. A word of encouragement, challenge, or confirmation from a trusted mentor can provide clarity.

Find a Spiritual Community

Joining a faith community creates space for encouragement, accountability, and growth. Proverbs 27:17 reminds us, "As iron sharpens iron, so one person sharpens another." Your calling is confirmed and strengthened when lived out in community.

4. Be Open to Change and God's Timing

Be Patient

Discerning a calling can take time. Moses waited forty years in the desert before leading Israel. David was anointed king years before he wore the crown. God's timing is always perfect.

Be Open to Unexpected Paths

God's call may come in surprising ways. What you thought was a setback may be His setup for something new. Isaiah 55:8 reminds us, "For my thoughts are not your thoughts, neither are your ways my ways, saith the Lord."

Take Intentional Action

Don't be paralyzed by indecision. Take small steps of faith and allow God to redirect you along the way. Obedience in little things prepares you for greater assignments.

5. Test the Calling

Compare it with Scripture

Does the calling align with biblical principles? God's call will never lead you into compromise but into holiness, service, and obedience.

Seek Confirmation

Ask God for confirmation through peace in your spirit, affirmation from others, and open doors that only He could create. Gideon sought signs, and God graciously gave them to strengthen his faith.

Be Willing to Obey

Once you believe God is calling you, be ready to act. Calling always requires a response. Abraham obeyed and went, not knowing where he was going (Hebrews 11:8). In the same way, you may not see the full picture, but faith requires moving forward step by step.

Final Encouragement

Discovering The Life You Were Created For ! is not about a one-time event, but about walking with God daily. As you seek Him, reflect on your passions, listen to wise counsel, remain open to His timing, and test everything by His Word, you will find that your steps are ordered by the Lord.

I Corinthians 1:26-31 ²⁶ For ye see your calling, brethren, how that not many wise men after the flesh, not many mighty, not many noble, are called: ²⁷ But God hath chosen the foolish things of the world to confound the wise; and God hath chosen the weak things of the world to confound the things which are mighty; ²⁸ And base things of the world, and things which are despised, hath God chosen, yea, and things which are not, to bring to nought things that are: ²⁹ That no flesh should glory in his presence. ³⁰ But of him are ye in Christ Jesus, who of God is made unto us wisdom, and righteousness, and sanctification, and redemption: ³¹ That, according as it is written, He that glorieth, let him glory in the Lord.

God can and will use any willing vessel!

Remember: Calling is less about what you *do* and more about *who you become* in Christ. When you align your life with Him, your calling will naturally unfold.

Bonus Chapter XXI

THE DEVIL CAN'T TAKE YOU OUT BECAUSE GOD'S GOT YOU!!

Romans 8
King James Version
I encourage you to read and meditate on each verse and draw strength, understanding, and guidance as you move into action with your divine calling.

1 There is therefore now no condemnation to them which are in Christ Jesus, who walk not after the flesh, but after the Spirit.

2 For the law of the Spirit of life in Christ Jesus hath made me free from the law of sin and death.

3 For what the law could not do, in that it was weak through the flesh, God sending his own Son in the likeness of sinful flesh, and for sin, condemned sin in the flesh: 4 That the righteousness of the law might be fulfilled in us, who walk not after the flesh, but after the Spirit.

5 For they that are after the flesh do mind the things of the flesh; but they that are after the Spirit the things of the Spirit.

6 For to be carnally minded is death; but to be spiritually minded is life and peace.

7 Because the carnal mind is enmity against God: for it is not subject to the law of God, neither indeed can be.

8 So then they that are in the flesh cannot please God.

9 But ye are not in the flesh, but in the Spirit, if so be that the Spirit of God dwell in you. Now if any man have not the Spirit of Christ, he is none of his.

10 And if Christ be in you, the body is dead because of sin; but the Spirit is life because of righteousness.

11 But if the Spirit of him that raised up Jesus from the dead dwell in you, he that raised up Christ from the dead shall also quicken your mortal bodies by his Spirit that dwelleth in you.

12 Therefore, brethren, we are debtors, not to the flesh, to live after the flesh. 13 For if ye live after the flesh, ye shall die: but if ye through the Spirit do mortify the deeds of the body, ye shall live.

14 For as many as are led by the Spirit of God, they are the sons of God.

15 For ye have not received the spirit of bondage again to fear; but ye have received the Spirit of adoption, whereby we cry, Abba, Father.

16 The Spirit itself beareth witness with our spirit, that we are the children of God: 17 And if children, then heirs; heirs of God, and joint-heirs with Christ; if so be that we suffer with him, that we may be also glorified together.

18 For I reckon that the sufferings of this present time are not worthy to be compared with the glory which shall be revealed in us.

19 For the earnest expectation of the creature waiteth for the manifestation of the sons of God.

20 For the creature was made subject to vanity, not willingly, but by reason of him who hath subjected the same in hope,

21 Because the creature itself also shall be delivered from the bondage of corruption into the glorious liberty of the children of God.

22 For we know that the whole creation groaneth and travaileth in pain together until now.

23 And not only they, but ourselves also, which have the firstfruits of the Spirit, even we ourselves groan within ourselves, waiting for the adoption, to wit, the redemption of our body.

24 For we are saved by hope: but hope that is seen is not hope: for what a man seeth, why doth he yet hope for?

25 But if we hope for that we see not, then do we with patience wait for it.

26 Likewise, the Spirit also helpeth our infirmities: for we know not what we should pray for as we ought: but the Spirit itself maketh intercession for us with groanings which cannot be uttered.

27 And he that searcheth the hearts knoweth what is the mind of the Spirit, because he maketh intercession for the saints according to the will of God.

28 And we know that all things work together for good to them that love God, who are called according to his purpose.

29 For whom he did foreknow, he also did predestinate to be conformed to the image of his Son, that he might be the firstborn among many brethren.

30 Moreover, whom he did predestinate, them he also called: and whom he called, them he also justified: and whom he justified, them he also glorified.

31 What shall we then say to these things? If God be for us, who can be against us?

32 He that spared not his own Son, but delivered him up for us all, how shall he not with him also freely give us all things?

33 Who shall lay anything to the charge of God's elect? It is God that justifieth.

34 Who is he that condemneth? It is Christ that died, yea rather, that is risen again, who is even at the right hand of God, who also maketh intercession for us.

35 Who shall separate us from the love of Christ? shall tribulation, or distress, or persecution, or famine, or nakedness, or peril, or sword?

36 As it is written, For thy sake we are killed all the day long; we are accounted as sheep for the slaughter.

37 Nay, in all these things we are more than conquerors through him that loved us.

38 For I am persuaded, that neither death, nor life, nor angels, nor principalities, nor powers, nor things present, nor things to come,

39 Nor height, nor depth, nor any other creature, shall be able to separate us from the love of God, which is in Christ Jesus our Lord.

By actively seeking God, reflecting on your gifts, and seeking wise counsel, you can discern the specific ways God is calling you to serve Him and make a difference in the world.

My mother, on her deathbed bed lay for hours almost lifeless, and as I sat holding her hand, out of nowhere, she nearly sat up in the bed, opening her eyes and seemingly looking into my eyes with a stern voice said, "LET NOTHING SHAKE YOUR FAITH". She never spoke another word to anyone before she met Jesus.

My friends, whatever you do from this moment on, always remember what Mama said:

"LET NOTHING SHAKE YOUR FAITH!"
Come on, you can do it!!!!

www.ingramcontent.com/pod-product-compliance
Lightning Source LLC
Chambersburg PA
CBHW051220120626
46547CB00013B/1437